THE GOD OF SMALL THINGS

Arundati Roy

AUTHORED by Tania Asnes
UPDATED AND REVISED by Adam Kissel

COVER DESIGN by Table XI Partners LLC
COVER PHOTO by Olivia Verma and © 2005 GradeSaver, LLC

BOOK DESIGN by Table XI Partners LLC

Published by GradeSaver LLC, www.gradesaver.com

First published in the United States of America by GradeSaver LLC. 2006

GRADESAVER, the GradeSaver logo and the phrase "Getting you the grade since 1999" are registered trademarks of GradeSaver, LLC

ISBN 978-1-60259-027-4

Printed in the United States of America

For other products and additional information please visit
http://www.gradesaver.com

Table of Contents

Table of Contents

Biography of Arundati Roy (1961-)

Arundhati Roy was born in 1961 in the Northeastern Indian region of Bengal, to a Christian mother and Hindu father. She spent her childhood in Aymanam in Kerala, which serves as the setting for her first novel, The God of Small Things (under the name Ayemenem). Roy s mother, Mary Roy, homeschooled her until the age of ten, when she began attending regular classes. She has been reluctant to discuss her father publicly, having spent very little time with him during her lifetime; Roy instead focuses on her mother s influence in her life. Mary Roy, a political activist, won an unprecedented victory for women s rights in Kerala. Through her persistence, the Supreme Court granted Christian women in Kerala the right to have an inheritance.

She spent her teenage years at boarding school in Southern India, after which she earned her degree from the School of Planning and Architecture in Delhi. After graduating, Roy supported herself by teaching aerobics while honing her writing skills. She eventually wrote several film scripts, which are recognized for their complex structure and biting social commentary. Roy wrote and starred in the film In Which Annie Gives It Those Ones, and she wrote the script for Electric Moon, directed by her second husband, Pradip Krishen. (Her first husband was Gerard Da Cunha, whom she met while in college. Their marriage lasted approximately four years.) Both films garnered a cult following, setting the stage for the fiction-writing side of Roy s career. Penguin published the script for In Which Annie Gives It Those Ones as a book in 2004.

Even when she was a low-profile writer, Roy began to assert her political opinions loudly. She rallied media support for Phoolan Devi, a politician and former criminal of Robin-Hood fame, whom she felt was being misrepresented by the film Bandit Queen (directed by Shekhar Kapur). After the controversy surrounding Bandit Queen subsided, Roy took time to write her first and only novel to date, The God of Small Things. She received an extraordinary advance of half a million pounds on the book, making its release high-profile well ahead of time. After the novel s publication in 1997, the book won the prestigious Booker Prize, making Roy its first Indian woman and non-expatriate Indian recipient.

In addition to her novelistic skills, Roy is widely known for political activism (perhaps along the lines of a Noam Chomsky). She has published many works of nonfiction including several essays as well as The End of Imagination (1998), The Greater Common Good (1999), The Cost of Living (1999), Power Politics (2002), War Talk (2003), The Checkbook and the Cruise Missile (2004, with David Barsamian), and An Ordinary Person s Guide to Empire (2004). She also took part in the June 2005 World Tribunal on Iraq. In January 2006 she was awarded the Sahitya Akademi award for her collection of essays, The Algebra of Infinite Justice, but she declined to accept it.

Roy has faced accusations of being anti-American and was convicted of contempt of court by the New Delhi Supreme Court for her political activism. She remains relentless. For instance, she was awarded the Sydney Peace Prize in 2004 for her efforts toward social justice and peaceful conflict resolution. Roy continues to write, engage in advocacy, and live with her husband in New Delhi.

About The God of Small Things

The God of Small Things is Arundhati Roy s first and only novel to date. It is semi-autobiographical in that it incorporates, embellishes, and greatly supplements events from her family s history. When asked why she chose Ayemenem as the setting for her novel, Roy replied, It was the only place in the world where religions coincide; there's Christianity, Hinduism, Marxism and Islam and they all live together and rub each other down I was aware of the different cultures when I was growing up and I'm still aware of them now. When you see all the competing beliefs against the same background you realize how they all wear each other down. To me, I couldn't think of a better location for a book about human beings." Because of her ingrained understanding of Ayemenem s diversity and cultural paradoxes, Roy allowed her imagination to run wild in a familiar landscape.

Upon finishing the novel in 1996 after four years of writing, Roy was offered an advance of half a million pounds. Rights to the book were demanded worldwide in 21 countries from India to New York. Upon its publication, the novel became a bestseller, going on to win England s premier literary award, the Booker Prize, in 1997. This made Roy the first Indian woman and non-expatriate to win the award.

Yet Roy s grand introduction into the fiction canon was not without incident. The God of Small Things infamously enraged some leftist Keralans upon its release. Soon after the book s release in 1997, a lawyer named Sabu Thomas attempted to have the book s last chapter removed because of its graphic description of sexual acts between members of different castes. Fortunately for the author and the novel, Thomas was unsuccessful and his lawsuit served only to bolster Roy s assertions throughout the novel that the caste system still greatly affects present-day Indian society.

Winning the Booker Prize placed Roy among the ranks of such writers as Salman Rushdie. Although in interviews Roy has denied imitating Rushdie s style, The God of Small Things certainly shows his influence. The novel's constantly changing perspective, its nonlinear progression of narrative, its lush, almost extravagant, sometimes capitalized or contracted diction, and its confounding of fantasy and reality also connect the novel with the style of hysterical realism (one might think here of the young American writer, Jonathan Safran Foer). Despite these similarities to others, Roy's narrative style and perspective are distinctive in The God of Small Things. In addition to the literary techniques described above, Roy hones a delicate use of language that makes each word seem precious while imbuing phrases with a keen sense of whimsy. She skillfully incorporates foreshadowing in tiny refrains such as Things can change in a day, roses sicksweet on a breeze, and blood spilling from his skull like a secret. The reader must collect these phrases along the way so that they fall into place with ease by the novel s end.

According to one critic, [Roy s] most original contribution in this novel is her portrayal of children, entering into their thinking in a way which does not sentimentalize them but reveals the fierce passions and terrors which course through them and almost destroy them.   Indeed, the perspectives of child protagonists Rahel and Estha are given the most weight of any throughout the novel. Even though, according to another critic, Rahel and Estha are   victims of circumstance,   they are to an equal extent intelligent evaluators of it.

Although the book has no single protagonist and no definitive moral, it certainly champions details of life to which contemporary society tends to be too frenzied or farsighted to pay heed. Roy does her best in the novel (as well as in her other writing and political activism) to enfranchise the "Small Things," overlooked people and issues that, in her opinion, deserve more attention.

Character List

Rahel

Estha's female fraternal twin. Much of the story is told from Rahel's perspective as a seven-year-old girl and as a thirty-one-year-old woman. She has an instinctive connecton to Estha, and as a child she could share experiences and memories with him unconsciously. She grows up in Ayemenem but, as an adult, lives in the United States with her husband, Larry McCaslin. After their divorce and upon hearing of her brother's return to Ayemenem, Rahel goes home herself.

Estha

Rahel's male fraternal twin. His full name is Esthappen. After Sophie Mol's death, he is sent to live with his father, Babu, in Assam. At the age of thirty-one, he moves back to Ayemenem. Estha stopped talking one day when he was a child and has not said a word since. He is considered crazy by the other inhabitants of Ayemenem except for Rahel.

Sophie Mol

The daughter of Chacko and Margaret Kochamma. After her stepfather Joe dies, she visits Ayemenem with her mother. She has "Pappachi's nose," but otherwise she looks decidedly Western compared to the rest of the family, with her light eyes and skin. She drowns in the Ayemenem river. Her death and the events surrounding it serve as a focus of the novel.

Ammu

Estha's and Rahel's mother. She married Babu in a glamorous ceremony, but she soon became disillusioned with their marriage because her husband was an alcoholic. After he tried to proposition her into sleeping with his boss, Ammu left Babu and settled back in Ayemenem with the twins. She has an affair with the Untouchable handyman, Velutha, so she is banished from her own house. She dies at the age of thirty-one while out of town on business.

Babu

Estha's and Rahel's father and Ammu's ex-husband. He is an alcoholic who is talked about but never seen in the novel. Estha lives with him when he works on a tea estate in Assam, but Babu cannot or will not take his son along to Australia.

Mammachi

Estha's and Rahel's blind grandmother. She is unhappily married to Pappachi, who beats her terribly until Chacko defends her. She plays the violin and generally keeps to herself, except when Ammu's and Velutha's affair is exposed.

Pappachi

Estha's and Rahel's grandfather. He beats Mammachi with a brass vase frequently, until Chacko forces him to stop. His prize in life is his sky-blue Plymouth. His biggest regret is not having the species of moth he discovered named after him.

Baby Kochamma

Rahel's and Estha's grandaunt. She has a degree in ornamental gardening, but in her old age she simply watches television and writes in her diary. Her life's biggest regret is not winning the affections of a priest, Father Mulligan. Baby Kochamma has a vindictive and manipulative personality; she accuses Velutha of raping Ammu and then pressures Estha to confirm it.

Chacko

Rahel's and Estha's uncle, and Mammachi's and Pappachi's only son. He was a Rhodes Scholar at Oxford, and he is now a card-carrying Communist. He took over Paradise Pickles & Preserves from Mammachi. Chacko's marriage to Margaret Kochamma crumbled after she could no longer stand his flabby, lazy nature. Even though he is separated from his ex-wife and daughter, he feels a strong affinity for them.

Velutha

An Untouchable Paravan who serves as a handyman for Ammu, Mammachi, and the rest of the family. He has a close relationship with Estha and Rahel, whom he treats lovingly but never condescendingly. He is the father figure they never had. Velutha has an affair with Ammu, rowing across the river to see her each night. After he is accused of raping Ammu and kidnapping the children, the police beat him nearly to death. They leave him to die in a prison cell, which he does, but not before Estha is tricked into confirming his guilt.

Vellya Paapen

Velutha's father and an old, fond acquaintance of Mammachi. When he discovers Velutha's affair with Ammu, he goes to Mammachi immediately and offers to kill Velutha with his bare hands in retribution for the shame he thinks Velutha has brought to Mammachi's family.

Kuttappen

Velutha's paralyzed brother. He helps Estha and Rahel figure out how to fix their boat.

Father Mulligan

A priest who is in Ayemenem when Baby Kochamma is a young woman. Despite her best efforts to impress him, Father Mulligan is not interested in Baby Kochamma. Eventually, he rejects the church to become a follower of Vishnu. He keeps in touch with Baby Kochamma until his death.

Kochu Maria

A tiny, pudgy house servant who, until the twins return, is the only other person living in the Ayemenem House with Baby Kochamma. She likes to watch wrestling on television and lives a sedentary lifestyle like her housemate.

Mr. Hollick

Babu s boss at the Assam tea estate. He gives Babu an ultimatum: lose his job or send Ammu to sleep with Mr. Hollick. Babu s attempt to get Ammu to comply is the last straw for her and is what leads to their divorce.

Larry McCaslin

Rahel's American ex-husband. He falls in love with and marries Rahel, but then he feels totally disconnected from her. Their marriage falls apart, and Rahel moves back to Ayemenem.

Joe

Margaret Kochamma's true love and Sophie Mol's stepfather. He dies in an accident, causing Margaret and Sophie to seek relief and refuge with their relatives in Ayemenem.

Comrade Pillai

Leader of the Communist Party in Ayemenem. He has a very intelligent son named Lenin. Comrade Pillai does not like the fact that Velutha is a Communist, because he does not want to be allied with him. In fact, he turns Velutha away on the night of his death and is therefore the last to see him before the police beat him.

Kochu Thomban

An elephant that sleeps in the temple while Rahel and Estha watch the Kathakali performance.

Murlidharan

A homeless, insane person who crouches naked on the welcome sign for Cochin. He carries the keys to his last residence around his waist expectantly.

Orangedrink Lemondrink man

The man at the concessions stand in the lobby of Abhilask Talkies. He molests Estha in the lobby while the rest of the family is watching *The Sound of Music*. The incident haunts Estha well into his adulthood.

Inspector Thomas Mathew

The police inspector who interviews Baby Kochamma on the night Velutha dies. He is somewhat ambivalent about his men's practices of beating Untouchables nearly to death without having a substantiated reason.

Major Themes

Small Things

In a society concerned with Big Things such as the caste system, political affiliations, and marriage, Roy directs the reader to the Small Things. These can be small creatures and their activities the whisper and scurry of small lives as well as secrets, promises, sins, and other emotional creatures that people do not want to acknowledge. All of these things seem to have no place in the lives of characters like Baby Kochamma and Comrade Pillai. They want to strive for culturally significant ideals such as an honorable family and a noble political life. Because Small Things are shunned, they must find refuge in dark, secret places like the river and the History House, or the hearts of those willing to nurture and protect them. It can be a good or bad thing to keep watch over Small Things. Velutha, The God of Small Things, slips from place to place undetected, enjoying life s small pleasures without paying attention to the Big fact that he is an Untouchable and should not be playing with the twins or sleeping with their mother. Velutha is also called The God of Loss, a sad title that references the loneliness that accompanies living amongst the Small Things. At the same time, recognizing the powerful presence of Small Things means knowing that we are never alone; there is always someone watching, even if it is a flea or even a microbe. Estha and Rahel are the the disciples of The God of Small Things. They explore the world of the river and History House, where no one else dares go. Because they are children, they are not as tied to the world of Big Things as the adults. Yet they also bear the brunt of the weight of the sad and dangerous Small Things that go on in their family s life: Estha s molestation, Rahel s fear that Ammu loves her a little less, the secret of what really happened to Sophie Mol, and the beating of Velutha, which they see with their own eyes. When Rahel and Estha make love as adults, they are finally letting go of their grief through action--they set themselves free from the burden of their Small Things.

The Grotesque

The grotesque permeates the story of The God of Small Things from the very beginning, when Rahel imagines the ceiling-painter dying on the floor, blood spilling from his skull like a secret. We learn later that this is Velutha, dying alone and wrongfully accused in the police station. The grotesque takes precedence throughout the story precisely because it is not allowed to do so by the characters. That is, it is the manifestation of the ugly secrets that the family refuses to acknowledge, and since they are forbidden from being acknowledged openly, they are forced to seep into the world of "Small Things" through language, dreams, and daydreams. Two repeating grotesque images are of Velutha s broken body and Sophie Mol s drowned corpse. They are the proverbial skeletons in the family s closet, willed to be nonexistent but unable to be forgotten. Therefore they become macabre images that haunt the characters, especially Rahel and Estha. Also, sex and violence are connected in a grotesque way in the novel. The first instance of this combination is in Estha's molestation; his first sexual experience is a terrifying violation. And when it is safe on the riverbank, Ammu's and Velutha's affair is crystallized and beautiful, but once it is discovered, it quickly becomes associated with violent death. Finally, when Estha and Rahel make love, their incest is grotesque. Roy portrays the act of lovemaking as beautiful, but it is made bizarre by the fact that Rahel and Estha are siblings--twins, no less--and that they are doing so out of "hideous grief." It is as though in order to overcome all their grotesque secrets, Rahel and Estha must perform a grotesque act.

Homecoming

The family members lives revolve around Ayemenem even though practically all of them journey away from it and then make a homecoming journey. The most prominent homecomings are those of Estha and Rahel. Estha comes home because he has nowhere else to go, and Rahel comes home to be with him. They come home to the place of their childhood and their deepest fears and pains, as well as to one another--they have not seen each other in thirty-one years. Throughout the story, we find the adult Rahel and Estha sharing space but not bridging the gap in their communication. When they finally break the rules and make love, they can finally feel as though they are back home, even as they violate a community norm. For them, the location of Ayemenem is not home so much as the safe haven within Ayemenem that they represent for one another. Other characters such as Baby Kochamma and Chacko leave India to study, but they too always end up back in Ayemenem. When Sophie and Margaret Kochamma arrive in Ayemenem, they are treated as though they are returning home. A cake is festooned with Welcome Home, Our Sophie Mol, and a matching song is sung. The family sees Sophie s homecoming as a part of the clan making a rightful return. Roy uses the theme of homecoming to explain that we cannot escape history and our roots. We can ignore it and relegate it to forbidden places like the History House and the pickle factory, but we will always "come home" to the reality of wo we are and what we have done in our lives. Nevertheless, two characters who do not get to come home before their deaths are Ammu and Velutha. They die outside their own worlds in foreign rooms. The fact that they do not make a homecoming journey is a testament to the fact that although they pay for their actions with their lives (or in Ammu s case, her life as she knows it), they do escape the bounds of their roots, namely their castes.

Scandal

Although they do their utmost to hide it, the family members' lives are filled with scandals. The foremost of these is Sophie Mol s death. Somehow the scandal of the incident is intensified by the fact that Sophie is not native to Ayemenem, so her death there is far out of the ordinary. Connected immediately to Sophie s death is Ammu's and Velutha s affair. From the moment it is discovered, the affair goes from a clandestine experience of pleasure to an act punishable by death. Even before the police all but kill Velutha, Vellya Paapen offers to kill him with his bare hands, and Mammachi banishes him from her property on pain of death. Estha s molestation by the Orangedrink Lemondrink man is a scandal acknowledged only by Rahel and Estha. There are also smaller scandals peppering the story, such as Velutha s affiliation with the Communist Party and the question of whether Sophie Mol is Chacko s legitimate child. The characters almost rely on scandal to make their lives interesting, but they continually banish scandals to the world of Small Things to the extent that they reemerge in unexpected, often grotesque ways.

Mutability

One of the refrains Roy uses in The God of Small Things is, Things can change in a day. This phrase encapsulates the tumultuousness of the characters lives; when change happens to them, it is usually on a large and enduring scale. Specifially, the story s three major deaths Sophie s, Velutha s, and Ammu s mark major points of change for all the characters. These deaths are focal points for the story they are bizarre, sudden occurrences that suggest the randomness of life in general and the notion that things as we know them are always in transition. Although the family would like to think that their individual secrets and desires can be preserved just as easily as pickles and jams, in fact life goes on developing whether it is acknowledged or not. Other major points of change in the novel are Estha s leaving Ayemenem to live with Babu, Estha s molestation by the Orangedrink Lemondrink man, the first time that Ammu realizes her attraction to Velutha, and the first time they meet by the river and make love.

Preservation

In contrast to her assertion that Things can change in a day, Roy also uses The God of Small Things to focus on the way that events and ideas are preserved. The world of Small Things is a quiet repository for those things that the world of Big Things finds unacceptable. These include small secrets and pains, like Ammu s knowledge that Ammu loves her a little less, bigger things like Estha s molestation by the Orangedrink Lemondrink man, or things so enormous that they are barely containable, like Ammu's and Velutha s affair and the story s three major deaths. Small things can change, but to look at the flip side of mutability, they also can be preserved. Instead of being acknowledged and worked through, these types of socially-uncomfortable topics are relegated to the safe, sacred, untouchable world of the riverbank and History House, thereby being bottled up. The family s business, Paradise Pickles & Preserves, embodies the family s desire to keep the secrets and scandals out of sight. As long as these things are kept under glass as the preserves and pickles literally are, they pose no threat. It is worth noting that the family does not own a cleaning or cremation operation their business is not in tidying or eliminating things, but in carefully locking them away to be enjoyed later. Scandal can make them miserable, but it also keeps their lives interesting. We see this especially with Baby Kochamma, who revels in stirring up scandal under the false pretense of trying to eliminate it. Of course, when a fruit or vegetable is pickled or preserved, its nature changes permanently; one would be as hard-pressed to reverse any of the family s scandals as turn a pickle back into a cucumber or illegal jam back into a banana. Once time has passed and a secret or scandal has been preserved, there is no way to go back and be sure of what exactly happened. Therefore the pickled secrets allow the characters lives to be intriguing but not wholly incriminating, painful, or understood. Unlike pickles, though, pickled scandals have a way of gaining in pressure until they burst out from their containers.

Cultural Loyalty

Roy has said that one of the things that brought her back to her childhood home of Ayemenem as the setting for her novel was the cultural diversity she remembers thriving amidst in her own life. When religions, cultures, and castes clash in Ayemenem, the results can range from minor disturbances to major acts of violence, as with Velutha s death. But there is also a certain beauty to such a kaleidoscopic range of people, which Roy suggests is worth the struggle for overall cultural cohesion. To a certain extent, all of the family members are anglophiles; Chacko, Baby Kochamma, and Rahel all get their educations in the Western tradition. Yet none of them renounces their own culture; they all return to Ayemenem. When Sophie Mol and Margaret Kochamma arrive in India, the family goes to lengths to anticipate what Western things might make them feel at home. The twins are encouraged to sing English songs, and a cake says Welcome Home, Our Sophie Mol in English. In the same way, Comrade Pillai tries to impress Chacko by having his children recite English poetry. Another cultural element in Ayemenem is Communist activity, which involves Comrade Pillai, Chacko, and Velutha. Even though they are politically affiliated, the caste system trumps any sense of brotherhood that Comrade Pillai would have with Velutha. He refuses to help him on the grounds that he is an Untouchable, although later he is happy to use Velutha s death as an excuse to agitate the workers of Paradise Pickles & Preserves. In her descriptions of the Cochin hotel and Kathakali dancers in the temple, Roy seems to mourn a certain cultural purity that is lost in Kerala s becoming a tourist location, God s Own Country. Historical buildings are turned into lounges and dining halls, and the beautiful and drawn-out art of Kathakali is abridged to suit tourists taste and patience. Luckily, cultural authenticity is one of the Small Things preserved in havens of Ayemenem such as the History House and the river.

Glossary of Terms

Ayemenem

An actual town in the Southern Indian state of Kerala, spelled "Aymanam." Arundhati Roy spent her childhood there, and it is the main setting for The God of Small Things.

Caste system

A social system that grades society based on castes, or classes. In India, the class system is hereditary and "stratified according to Hindu ritual purity." The highest caste are Brahmans and the lowest are Untouchables.

Cochin

A major city in the South Indian state of Kerala, which hosts the region's major airport. It is where the family goes to greet Sophie Mol and Margaret Kochamma upon their arrival from England. Because Cochin is a tourist city, its history has been shelved in favor of pleasing foreigners: historical rooms are turned into lobbies and dining rooms, and traditional Kathakali performances are abridged and catered to tourist-level patience and taste.

Communist

A follower of communism, often as expressed in the philosophy of Karl Marx and the politics of Lenin. It is often seen as subversive by non-Communists for its revolutionary, levelling spirit. Comrade Pillai, Chacko, and Velutha are all card-carrying Communists.

Comrade

A fellow member of the Communist Party.

Coolie

In Asia, an offensive word for an unskilled laborer.

History House

The abandoned house across the river, where Velutha lives with Vellya Paapen and Kuttappen. Estha and Rahel become obsessed with the History House and use the shadowy area surrounding it as their haven from the Ayemenem House. It is the History House to which they run away after Ammu calls them burdens.

Kathakali

A traditional art form native to Kerala, which combines opera, dance, and "full-body acting." It makes use of Malayalam literature and mudras as well as elaborate costuming and makeup in order to portray regional legends. Rahel and Estha watch an authentic Kathakali performance in the temple. But in tourist spots such as Cochin, the Kathakali performances, traditionally several hours long, are abridged to please the foreigners' patience and taste.

Kerala

One of the four states comprising Southern India, located on the southwest tip of India, bordered to the west by the Arabian Sea and on the east by the Ghat Mountains. Save flashbacks, the entire story of The God of Small Things unfolds in Kerala.

Paravan

A low, untouchable caste, usually of fishermen. Velutha and his family are Paravans. As with any caste, being a Paravan is hereditary.

The Grotesque

A style of literature and/or art in which things are distorted and made bizarre. It can incorporate the supernatural, violence, the unmentionable, and sexuality.

Untouchables

Those in the caste system who are at the bottom. They are considered unclean, especially by the more "pure" upper castes. Roy seems to incorporate the meaning of "untouchable" in the sense of "irreproachable," suggesting that what is untouchable may also be sacred. Velutha and his relatives are considered Untouchables.

Short Summary

The God of Small Things tells the story of one family in the town of Ayemenem in Kerala, India. Its epigraph is a quotation from contemporary writer John Berger: Never again will a single story be told as though it s the only one. She uses this idea to establish her nonlinear, multi-perspective way of storytelling, which gives value to points of view as Big as a human being s and as Small as a cabbage-green butterfly s. In Roy s world, there is no definitive story, only many different stories that fuse to form a kaleidoscopic impression of events.

The novel opens with Rahel s return to Ayemenem after hearing that her twin brother, Estha, has come home. We switch to the funeral of Sophie Mol, when the twins are seven years old. Rahel believes that Sophie is awake during her funeral and buried alive. The rest of the family refuses to acknowledge the twins and Ammu. On the train ride back to Ayemenem, Ammu cannot speak except to say He s dead I ve killed him. Rahel and Estha have not seen each other since Estha was sent away as a child to live with Babu in Assam. Both twins have traveled somewhat aimlessly until returning to their childhood home. Rahel looks out on the family s former factory, Paradise Pickles & Preserves, and contemplates how all the strangeness in her family resolves around the incident of Sophie Mol s death.

Next, we find the family traveling to Cochin to greet Sophie Mol and her mother, Margaret Kochamma, upon their arrival from England. On their way, they see their servant, Velutha, marching with a group of Communists. Back in the present, Rahel watches Estha undress in the moonlight, neither of them saying a word.

The narrative returns to Cochin, where the family goes to see *The Sound of Music* in the cinema. Inside the theater, Estha cannot stop singing, so he is sent out into the lobby, where the Orangedrink Lemondrink man molests him. After he becomes nauseated, the family leaves the movie early. Rahel senses that the Orangedrink Lemondrink man has wronged Estha and talks back to Ammu when she praises the man. Ammu tells her that she loves Rahel a little less, a statement that haunts Rahel for a long time.

Back in the present, Rahel runs into Comrade Pillai, and he shows her a photograph of the twins and Sophie, taken shortly before Sophie died. In a flashback to Sophie s arrival at the Cochin airport, Rahel cannot handle the nervousness surrounding her cousin s arrival, and she is scolded for hiding in the window curtain. Everyone tries to impress Sophie and Margaret Kochamma with new clothing, English sayings, and forced upbeat attitudes.

The narrative turns to Ammu s death at the age of thirty-one. After being banished from the Ayemenem House, she dies while out of town on a job interview. Estha watches her body being pushed into the cremation oven. No one writes to Estha to inform him of Ammu s death. Roy introduces the refrain, Things can change in a day.

Back at Sophie Mol s welcome ceremony, a crowd gathers to sing and eat cake. Rahel retreats to play with Velutha. As Ammu watches her daughter and handyman together, she is attracted to Velutha for the first time.

Rahel joins Estha, who is alone in the pickle factory. They plan to visit the History House, where the Paravans live. They push an old, decrepit boat into the river and row to Velutha s side of the river. There, he promises to fix the boat for them. Velutha is trying to suppress his growing love for Ammu despite his constant association with her children. (Ammu dreams of a one-armed man making love to her.)

Back in the present, Rahel watches fondly as Estha bathes in the moonlight. The twins meet by coincidence at a temple, where they watch kathkali dancers act out a violent story of retribution all night.

We turn to the story of Chacko's and Magaret Kochamma s marriage. It began happily but soon crumbled because of a sense of disconnection. Margaret left Chacko for Joe, who later died in an accident. After that, she took Sophie to Ayemenem as a distraction; she can never forgive herself for leaving Sophie alone in Ayemenem the day she died.

We finally hear the story of Sophie Mol s death and the events surrounding it. Vellya Paapen comes to Mammachi s door and offers to kill Velutha with his bare hands for having an affair with Ammu. Baby Kochamma makes sure that Ammu is locked in her room and that the police think he raped Ammu. Mammachi summons Velutha to her house and fires him, banishing him from the property on pain of death. He goes to Comrade Pillai for help but to no avail. Roy begins to call Velutha The God of Loss and The God of Small Things. The telling of Sophie s actual death is short. She joins the twins as they run away after Ammu insults them terribly. After their boat capsizes in the river, she drowns. The twins fall asleep on the veranda of the History House, unaware that Velutha is sleeping there. The next morning, the police come across the river to arrest Velutha. They beat him nearly to death and take the twins to the station with them. There, Baby Kochamma pressures Estha into saying Velutha is guilty of kidnapping him and Rahel. She tells him that doing so is the only way to save Ammu and avoid a life in jail. Estha complies, thus saving Baby Kochamma from being arrested for filing a false report about Velutha. After that, Baby Kochamma coerces Chacko into evicting Ammu from the house and forcing Estha to go live with Babu. As Estha leaves on the train, Rahel cries as though a part of her is being ripped out of her body.

Back in the present, Estha and Rahel finally share a fond moment in Ammu s former bedroom. They make love out of hideous grief for the deaths of Ammu, Velutha, and Sophie Mol.

The final chapter describes the first night of Ammu's and Velutha s affair. They are both drawn to the riverbank, where they meet and make love for the first time. After that, they continue to meet in secret and share their admiration of Small Things such as the creatures of the riverbank. Each night as they part, they say to one another: Tomorrow? Tomorrow. On the last night they meet before Velutha s death, Ammu is compelled to turn back and repeat one more time: Tomorrow.

Summary and Analysis of Chapters 1-3

Chapter 1 - Paradise Pickles & Preserves

The scene opens on the town of Ayemenem in the southern Indian province of Kerala. The setting is almost unbearably abundant and full of life. We encounter Rahel, who returns home to Ayemenem to see her twin brother, Estha. Still living in the same house is her grandaunt, Baby Kochamma. Rahel and Estha have a peculiar relationship. As children they considered themselves to be one person. Roy tells us that they were a rare breed of Siamese twins, physically separate, but with joint identities. Rahel used to share experiences, dreams, and memories with Estha. But as 31-year-old adults, the twins have become individual emotionally as well as physically. As young children they lived in the famous tea province of Assam. Later on, their parents divorced and Ammu returned to live in Ayemenem.

The narrative turns to the funeral of Sophie Mol, Rahel's and Estha's cousin. Sophie drowned at the age of nine while visiting Ayemenem from England. Rahel and Estha were seven years old at the time. Among those in attendance were Sophie's parents, Margaret Kochamma and Chacko, Baby Kochamma, and Rahel's and Estha's blind grandmother, Mamachi. Ammu, Rahel, and Estha had to stand separately from the rest of the family, and no one acknowledged their presence. Rahel was unusually aware of the small things going on during the funeral; she believed that that Sophie Mol was awake during the funeral and showed Rahel two things. The first was the unusual paintwork on the ceiling of the cathedral; it showed a blue sky complete with clouds and tiny airplanes. Rahel imagined the artist who painted it falling from his perch and cracking his head open, dark blood spilling from his skull like a secret. The second thing was a baby bat that crawled up Baby Kochamma's sari and may have bit her. Rahel saw Sophie Mol do a secret cartwheel in her coffin when this happened. Rahel also heard Sophie's screams when they buried her alive, according to Rahel. After the funeral, Estha and Rahel went with Ammu to the police station, where Ammu told the officer that there had been a terrible mistake. The officer was rude to Ammu and prodded her breasts. On the train ride back to Ayemenem, Ammu was in a trance and could say only He's dead I've killed him. Two weeks later, Baba forced Ammu to send Estha to live with him in Calcutta.

Rahel and Estha have not seen each other since; they have spent twenty-three years apart. But now Estha has returned to Ayemenem; Baba moved to Australia and could not take his son along. Estha walks alone in the rain. We learn that he stopped talking as a child and learned to blend into his surroundings so that he occupied very little space in the world, leading a withdrawn, mediocre existence. After graduating from school, he mortified Babu and his stepmother by doing the housework instead of going to college. He began a habit of taking long walks by himself. But once Rahel returned to Ayemenem, suddenly the world's noise infiltrated Estha's thoughts.

Rahel herself was wandering from school to school after Ammu died. As a child, she was expelled from three schools for her curiosity and inappropriate behavior. She attended architectural college in Delhi for eight years, never making the effort to graduate because she found the lifestyle comfortable. Her architectural designs were artless and impractical. She met her husband, Larry McCaslin, and immigrated to the United States with him. Their marriage crumbled from a sense of disconnection. When Rahel found out that Estha had returned to Ayemenem, she too returned home.

We next learn about Baby Kochamma, whose interesting life story belies her current, lazy existence. When she was eighteen, she fell in love with a visiting Irish monk, Father Mulligan. He was working with her father, Reverend John Ipe, who was famous for having been touched by the church Patriarch. Baby Kochamma tried to seduce Father Mulligan by pretending to be interested in religion and even joining a convent. When she realized that her attempts were in vain, she instead attended the University of Rochester in New York, graduating much heavier and with a degree in Ornamental Gardening. When she returned to the house in Ayemenem she kept a marvelous garden, which grew wild from neglect when she discovered her stronger love for television. This love she now shares with the midget housekeeper, Kochu Maria. Baby Kochamma is anxious now that the twins are back in Ayemenem, worrying as though they will steal the house from her.

Rahel looks out on her grandmother s old pickle factory, Paradise Pickles & Preserves. She remembers that the government banned their banana jam for being unclassifiable as either jam or jelly. She considers how this event encapsulates her family s way of life, which involves constantly transgressing different types of boundaries. In particular, she thinks about the mystery and uncomfortable atmosphere surrounding Estha s being sent away from Ayemenem. He carried with him a terrible memory of looking into the face of a beloved young man with an old man s mouth and saying Yes. Rahel considers that the strangeness in the family can be traced back to Sophie Mol s death, or perhaps all the way back to a time when India was yet uncolonized by the British.

Chapter 2 - Pappachi s Moth

The scene opens in December 1969. Rahel's and Estha s grandmother, Mammachi, is driving Rahel and Estha to Cochin for a vacation with Sophie Mol and Margaret Kochamma. Ammu, Chacko, and Baby Kochamma ride in the car as well. It is a sky-blue Plymouth that belonged to Pappachi. None of them besides Chacko has ever met Sophie Mol. As she sits in the car, Ammu, now twenty-seven, considers that it was a mistake to have married Babu. She met him at the age of eighteen while at a friend s wedding reception in Calcutta. He proposed to her after five days, and they were married in a luxurious ceremony. They moved to Assam, where he assistant-managed a tea estate. Babu turned out to be an alcoholic, and their marriage was unglamorous. The twins were born during the war with China in 1962. When they were twelve, Babu s boss, Mr. Hollick, gave him an ultimatum. He could either be fired for his laziness or send Ammu over to Mr. Hollick s bungalow to sleep with him. Babu tried to force Ammu to fulfill this proposition, and she beat him senseless before returning to Ayemenem with the twins. She became a beautiful but withdrawn and unpredictable person.

We next learn about Mammachi. When Pappachi was alive, she started her pickle business without his help. He used to beat her every night with a brass vase. When Chacko was home on summer vacation from Oxford, he threatened his father so that he never beat Mammachi again. To regain his pride, Pappachi bought the Plymouth and refused to let anyone else ride in it. Pappachi had been an Imperial Entomologist at the Pusa Institute in Delhi, and his biggest regret was that the moth he discovered was not named after him. It flew into his drink one day and, when he noticed its unusual appearance, he took it to the Pusa Institute. It was identified as a variant of a common species. But twelve years later, it was classified as a separate species, but Pappachi received no acknowledgment as its discoverer. After that, Pappachi became increasingly unpleasant and temperamental until he died of a heart attack.

The story turns to Chacko s relationship with the twins. Chacko told them that in order to understand their family, they had to visit the forbidden History House on the other side of the river. He also told them that the earth was an ancient Earth Woman, compared to whom they were inconsequential. Estha and Rahel became fascinated and haunted by how history permeated the present.

Back in the present, Chacko and Ammu argue in the car. Chacko is an eccentric Oxford Rhodes scholar who builds model airplanes as a hobby. He returned to Ayemenem after quitting his job as lecturer at Madras Christian College and took over the pickle business. Estha and Rahel read the road signs backwards, continuing a habit of reading both backwards and forwards that used to stymie their teacher, Ms. Mitten. The Plymouth passes the armless, naked lunatic, Murlidharan, on the way to Cochin. (Murlidharan lost his arms in Singapore in 1942. Ever since, he has wandered from place to place with the keys to his old home tied expectantly around his waist.) They drive through a procession of Communists. Chacko is an unofficial Communist, but the rest of the family tries to ignore the to-do. Rahel notices Velutha marching with the Communists. She rolls down the window and calls to him, producing an angry slap from Ammu.

We turn to Rahel living in New York, remembering this incident. She still does not understand why Ammu was so furious. Velutha was a Paravan like his father, Vellya Paapen, considered an Untouchable. But he was such a skilled craftsman that Mammachi let him do all kinds of chores for her. Then Velutha disappeared for four years. After he returned, he did maintenance in the pickle factory. The twins loved him. One day Vellya Paapen went to Mammachi and offered to kill Velutha with his own hands because he had seen Velutha rowing across the lake every night and returning every morning.

We return to the Communist marchers. They open the door of the Plymouth and make Baby Kochamma wave a Communist flag and repeat a slogan. Rahel concedes that it was not Velutha she saw after all. But after that day, Baby Kochamma antagonizes Velutha because of her shame at having been embarrassed. As the family continues to drive, Chacko says that Ammu, Estha, and Rahel are burdens to him. Outside the car, life goes on as usual despite the uncomfortable stillness and silence in the car.

Chapter 3 - Big Man the Laltain, Small Man the Mombatti

Baby Kochamma and Kochu Maria have let the house in Ayemenem become very dirty and unkempt. They watch television and eat nuts from a bowl as if it is a competition. There was an old coolie who used to meet Estha s school trip party at the train platform and carry their luggage. He would say: Big Man the Laltain, Small Man the Mombatti, meaning: Big Man the Lantern, Small Man the Tallow-Stick. Back in the present, a drenched Estha arrives at the door of the house, and Rahel follows him into Ammu s old room. He seems not to notice her as he undresses. She watches him with fascination, unashamed of his nakedness, admiring his body. Suddenly she reaches out to wipe a raindrop from his ear. As though he does not notice her, he begins to wash his clothes in silence.

Analysis

As soon as the novel opens, we are swept up into Ayemenem s excessive lushness. Roy begins by describing the setting as physically lush. She adeptly magnifies this effect by making excessive use of modifiers. Her diction is open, throaty, and watery in order to evoke a very sensual and also sexual mood. Roy uses language of abundance: gorge, burst, hum, sloth. She also makes her own compound words to give the sense that everything is clinging together: dustgreen, mossgreen. In addition, Roy immediately personifies the setting; for example, she writes: the countryside turned an immodest green. (Nature cannot be immodest since it does not have human consciousness.) This personification connects Roy s description of Ayemenem s natural world with its human inhabitants. It suggests that sexuality pervades the human world of Ayemenem in an illicit, sneaky way just as it does the natural world. In Ayemenem, nature sneaks through the crevices of manmade structures in order to find its full, sensuous glory: Boundaries blur as tapioca fences take root and bloom. Brick walls turn mossgreen. Pepper vines snake up electric poles. Wild creepers burst through laterite banks and spill across flooded roads Small fish appear in the puddles that fill the PWD potholes on the highways. So from the very beginning, Roy gives us the sense that there is a rebellious sexual energy in Ayemenem s society that is difficult to suppress despite the strict Indian caste system. Roy also attunes us to the small things, which she calls the whisper and scurry of small lives. She gives them value immediately, affirming the title s suggestion that by engaging in Roy s world, we are made to look past the larger realities of life in order to examine the influence of its minor details.

In the first three chapters, Roy establishes Sophie Mol s death as a focal point for the rest of the story. For the whole family and especially for Estha and Rahel, it is an event around which everything else revolves and to which everything connects. The centrality of Sophie Mol s death, or any death, makes us aware of the novel s focus on the grotesque. The grotesque is one of Roy s most important themes throughout the novel, and it is connected to sex as much as to violence. For instance, the melancholy mood of Ammu's and Babu s relationship culminates with a grotesque show of sexuality Babu tries to make Ammu sleep with his boss and violence, when Ammu beats Babu senseless for doing so. There is no instance of rape or what we would call "sexual violence," but sex and violence are intimately connected in this scene. The grotesque also appears somewhat randomly in the macabre thoughts of Rahel and the other characters. Grotesque already is Rahel s conviction that Sophie Mol is mourned and buried alive. In Roy s world, we might classify this as a Big Thing. Also grotesque are the Small Things at the funeral, which Sophie supposedly shows Rahel. These are the baby bat and the beautifully painted ceiling. Even the latter, which is wondrous and exquisite, is connected with a terrible sense of things gone wrong. Rahel is not a normal child; her thoughts wander into dark and very adult places. Therefore when she looks at the painted ceiling, her thoughts wander to the possible death of the man who must have painted them, dark blood spilling from his skull like a secret.

Rahel shares her ability to think dark thoughts with Estha. Although the twins have an uncanny, subconscious connection, they are also very different. Rahel is outwardly expressive and awkward for all her quiet contemplation, while Estha is decidedly even-keeled and solemn. Roy describes him as a quiet bubble floating on a sea of noise. Both twins are keen observers of the world around them, but they easily confuse fantasy with reality, as Rahel does at Sophie Mol s funeral. Their connection to one another traverses not only the normal boundaries of human communication, but also those of social appropriateness. At the end of Chapter 3, Rahel is not the least bit ashamed to watch, even to admire, her naked adult brother. In turn, he is not ashamed to be naked in front of her, and he goes about his activities as usual. As we learn later, the twins are not exempt from the persistent, socially-inappropriate sexual tide that rises in most members of the family. Another example of this is Baby Kochamma. In her old age, she seems to be a simple character who watches television and revels in being in control of the Ayemenem House. But after an insight into her past, we see that like Estha, Rahel, Ammu, Mammachi, and Chacko alike, she is sexually and romantically dissatisfied. She could not have Father Mulligan as she hoped, and she was unhappy alone just as Ammu was with Babu, Mammachi was with Pappachi, and Chacko is without Margaret Kochamma.

If marriages count as Big Things in the world of Ayemenem, then they are what force the members of the family to seek pleasure instead in the Small Things, those things that go unrecognized by society. Unable to have Father Mulligan, Baby Kochamma becomes obsessed with the Small Thing of writing to him in her diary; Ammu must make the love of her life a Small Thing, hidden on the riverbank away from others eyes. Ironically, sometimes Small Things achieve more recognition than Big Things. In the case of Pappachi and his moth, the latter, a Small Thing, achieves a place in history while its rightful discoverer is given no credit at all. As the coolie suggests, Small Things are the driving force behind all action. He says, Big Man the Lantern, Small Man the Tallow-Stick. Although the lantern magnifies the light, it is the tallow-stick that provides it. In the same way, although the big things in life usually get most of the attention, the small things provide much of the impetus behind everything that happens. The family members, being human, like to think that they have control over the events in their lives. But it is their secrets, carefully hidden away like their pickles and preserves, which really have the influence.

Summary and Analysis of Chapters 4-6

Chapter 4 - Abhilash Talkies

The family arrives at Abhilash Talkies, the cinema in Cochin. In the women s bathroom, Baby Kochamma, Ammu, and Rahel all urinate in front of one another. Rahel cherishes this intimacy. Alone in the men s bathroom, Estha stands on top of cans in order to be tall enough to urinate like a grown man at the urinal. This makes him proud. Then the family reunites and enters the movie theater. Estha cannot help but sing during the movie, which annoys the rest of the audience greatly. He leaves and heads for the lobby, where he annoys the refreshments seller, the Orangedrink Lemondrink man, with his singing. Then the man makes him come behind the counter for a free drink. He makes Estha fondle his penis while he drinks his drink. Then he sends him back into the theater, but Estha is nauseated. Ammu takes him to the ladies room. Back in the lobby, the Orangedrink Lemondrink man flirts with Ammu and gives Estha free sweets. Ammu notices that Estha is out of sorts, so she makes the family leave the movie early. Back in the lobby, Rahel senses that the Orangedrink Lemondrink man is not to be trusted. When Ammu praises him, Rahel retorts, So why don t you marry him then? only to be told that now Ammu loves her a little less. After that, Rahel is inconsolable and anxious, unable to forget Ammu s words.

They drive to the hotel, where Chacko wonders what his daughter, Sophie Mol, looks like. He remembers that before he and Margaret Kochamma divorced, he used to sneak into Sophie s room to memorize her face, wondering if she was really his child. In another room, Estha awakes and vomits into the toilet. Then he goes to Rahel s door; she senses him there and lets him in. Rahel wonders if it was indeed Velutha whom she saw marching with the Communists. She thinks about how Comrade K.N.M. Pillai, the local Communist leader, rallied the workers of Paradise Pickles to the Communist cause. Velutha was the only card-carrying Communist in the factory, and Comrade Pillai did not want to be allied with an Untouchable. In his hotel bed, Chacko considers how he might get around Comrade Pillai s attempts to rally his workers. In the next bed, Estha and Rahel hold each other and dream of the river near their house.

Chapter 5 - God s Own Country

The scene opens with a focus on the river, which has a history of its own. People over the generations bathe in, ride on, and defecate in it. It is unfit for swimming and has a nasty smell, but the people who own the nearby hotel tout the area as God s Own Country. At the hotel, history is twisted and abbreviated. Historical houses are converted into dining rooms and sitting areas, while traditional performances are abridged to suit tourists patience. Rahel runs into Comrade Pillai while walking around Ayemenem. After making small talk, he remembers something about a sex scandal and death in her family. He shows her a pile of photographs of his son, who is named Lenin. Rahel remembers the moment when Lenin became real for her and Estha. They were in the waiting room of a doctor s office, Rahel and Lenin both with foreign objects lodged in their noses. Afraid of the doctor, Rahel tried one last time to blow the glass bead out of her nose--and succeeded. Meanwhile, Lenin had to wait for the doctor to remove the object from his nose. Back in the present, Comrade Pillai shows Rahel a picture of herself, Estha, Lenin, and Sophie Mol. Rahel remembers that Sophie had made herself look silly for the picture, adorning herself whimsically and making a funny face. Just before the picture was taken, she had explained to Estha and Rahel that there was a good chance they were all illegitimate children. The picture was taken days before she died.

Chapter 6 - Cochin Kangaroos

The scene opens onto Cochin Airport on the day when Sophie Mol is scheduled to arrive. As Ammu helps Rahel get dressed in her new clothing, Rahel cannot help but remember that her mother loves her a little less for what she said the previous day. At the airport, the family is dressed in new, special clothing for Sophie s arrival. They hold welcome signs, and Ammu reminds the twins that they are ambassadors of India insofar as Sophie Mol is concerned. Sophie Mol and Margaret Kochamma arrive. The air is uncomfortable as Chacko greets his ex-wife and daughter. Sophie is taller than Estha and Rahel, with blue eyes, light skin, and dark brown hair. Baby Kochamma tells Sophie that she reminds her of Ariel from *The Tempest*, but Sophie does not understand the reference. Rahel hides in the window curtain because she is overwhelmed, but Ammu yells at her for having dirtied her dress. The children begin to get acquainted. On the car ride back, Estha and Rahel sing a song in English to impress Sophie. The chapter ends with the remark: Just outside Ayemenem they drove into a cabbage-green butterfly (or perhaps it drove into them).

Analysis

The theme of the grotesque deepens as the Orangedrink Lemondrink man molests Estha in Abhilash Talkies. Estha loses not only his innocence but his sense of safety. From that moment on, he is afraid that the man will seek him out to hurt him again. In the beginning of the novel, Roy tells us that the reason Estha stops talking is lost in history. Yet his encounter with the Orangedrink Lemondrink man seems a likely impetus. What leads up to the molestation is just the opposite of keeping quiet; Estha cannot stop singing in the movie theater, so he is sent out to the lobby where he falls prey to the bored, perverted predator. Estha s trauma silences him well into his adult years and perhaps forever. We encounter the adult Estha several times in the novel, but we never once hear him speak.

Rahel too loses her sense of safety as a result of Estha s molestation, although indirectly. Because of their subconscious connection, Rahel senses immediately that the Orangedrink Lemondrink man has done something terrible to Estha. But in their family, the big issues lurk just beneath the surface. They are not allowed to be acknowledged without disaster. Therefore Rahel s reaction, instead of telling Ammu her impression of the Orangedrink Lemondrink man, is to talk back to her. When Ammu tells her that she loves her a little less for hurting her, Rahel is inconsolable.

A little less her mother loved her becomes a refrain throughout the next several chapters. This statement, which is a Small Thing to Ammu, consumes Rahel. When Sophie arrives, Rahel thinks of her as Loved from the Beginning loved irrevocably whereas she is imperfect and Ammu s love for her is volatile.

The theme of cultural loyalty arrives along with Sophie Mol and Margaret Kochamma. They represent the foreign and exciting, but also that which does not belong. At the hotel, history is manipulated until it is suitably attractive to foreign eyes: historical buildings and rooms are converted into lounging and dining areas and traditional kathkali dances, famous for their all-night length, are abridged to less than an hour. Cultures are combined, resulting in strange hybrids that are authentic in the eyes of no one except perhaps a tourist. Sophie encapsulates this process by her appearance alone: she has Pappachi s nose, but her skin is light and her eyes are blue. She seems neither English nor Indian, and for this reason she is both fascinating and threatening. Back in Ayemenem, the History House serves as a haven for what is true but not necessarily attractive in the family s history. For this reason it is seen as forbidden and as untouchable like the people who live in it (Velutha, Vellya Paapen, and Kuttappen).

Just as the History House is a haven for history, the river and riverbank are havens for Small Things whether they are creatures or emotions. The inner workings of the natural world thrive there, as do other things overlooked by society such as Estha s fear of the Orangedrink Lemondrink man, the Paravans, Ammu's and Velutha s affair, and Sophie s death. In fact, the river does such a good job at keeping secrets that the latter two events remain hidden in tantalizing allusions until the novel s end--only then does Roy let us witness them firsthand. Just like the Paravans who live beyond the river, the Small Things in the river s domain are untouchable. They are so not because they are dirty or insignificant. These things are untouchable in the sense of being sacred. They cannot be ruined by society so long as they are kept separate and clandestine.

The last line of chapter 6 continues this theme of Small Things. Roy writes: Just outside Ayemenem they drove into a cabbage-green butterfly (or perhaps it drove into them). Not only does she take a moment (the last of a chapter, no less) to acknowledge something small, but she uses the moment to question the characters as well as the reader s perspective. In her parenthetical remark, Roy acknowledges that the human perspective or in a broader sense, the conventional perspective of the observer is far from the only one. Even a fragile insect can have a point of view and even a suicidal intention.

Summary and Analysis of Chapters 7-9

Chapter 7 - Wisdom Exercise Notebooks

Rahel searches for hidden things in Pappachi s study. Estha stands silently at the door. Rahel produces their childhood notebooks from a shelf and reads from Estha s, laughing at his childish mistakes as well as the fact that he chose to write about morbid topics.

We skip over to the last time Ammu returned to Ayemenem. The twins were nearly eleven, but only Rahel was at home. Ammu talked nonstop, as though talking would make the reality that she was dying disappear. Rahel hated Ammu during this time, and she never saw her again before her death. Ammu died at the age of thirty-one while out of town for a job interview. The church refused to bury her, so she was cremated. Rahel watched with Chacko while her body was pushed into the oven, but neither of them cried. Rahel never wrote to Estha to inform him of Ammu s death. To her, writing a letter to Estha was tantamount to writing a letter to a part of her body.

Back in the present, Rahel notices that Estha has left the doorway. She walks onto the veranda, where she sees him disappearing on another walk. She considers the fact that she is standing in the same spot where "Welcome home, Our Sophie Mol was performed. The chapter ends with the assertion that Things can change in a day.

Chapter 8 - Welcome Home, Our Sophie Mol

Mammachi plays the violin on the veranda while thinking about other things. When her mind wanders to Margaret Kochamma, her playing becomes angry. She hates Margaret Kochamma because things did not work out between her and Chacko, who is the recipient of all her adoration towards men, even though he is her son. Mammachi thinks of Margaret Kochamma as just another whore. Kochu Maria festoons a cake with the words: Welcome Home, Our Sophie Mol. Sophie Mol is greeted at the house by a crowd and a nervous, excited air. Everyone is showing excellent behavior, pretending that they live cheery, entertaining lives. As Roy puts it, And once again, only the Small Things were said. The Big Things lurked unsaid inside. Ammu watches as Rahel leaves the festivities to greet Velutha. Ammu admires Velutha s chiseled body and his familiar relationship with her daughter. Suddenly Velutha catches Ammu s glance and, for the first time, notices that she is a woman. The moment catches them both off guard and excites them. Back at the house, Ammu storms into her room after Margaret Kochamma accidentally insults her. She expresses fascination at Kochu Maria s way of kissing Sophie Mol s hands, which Ammu finds condescending. Ammu s touchy nature comes from having suffered Pappachi s terrible abuse throughout her childhood. While everyone has cake, she calls Rahel into the house and tells her not to be so close with Velutha. Rahel goes outside to squash ants and ignores Sophie Mol s attempts to play with her.

Chapter 9 - Mrs. Pillai, Mrs. Eapen, Mrs. Rajagopalan

The adult Rahel observes toads near the house in Ayemenem. She remembers a day when she and Estha took Sophie Mol to visit Velutha. She realizes how sweetly he entertained them as children, not judging them like their parents or trying to be a child himself just letting them be themselves. Rahel sees Estha in his room. Both of the twins feel lost in their lives, haunted by memories and bottled anger, left behind by Ammu to [spin] in the dark, with no moorings, in a place with no foundation. Again there is a vague reference to Sophie Mol s death. Rahel wanders to the abandoned pickle factory. She thinks of how on the day Sophie Mol arrived, Estha thought his Two Thoughts and hid a secret in a pickle jar. The chapter closes on the refrain: Things can change in a day.

Analysis

Chapters 7 and 8 deal with Ammu s death, but they also mock the idea of death because like the rest of the story, they do not follow a traditional, linear order. Death is the logical and inevitable end to life. But in Roy s world, things are illogical and unpredictable. The story of Ammu s death, then, unfolds in a nonlinear fashion. First we witness her cremation, the final affirmation that she is no longer living, then flash back to the moment when she begins to come alive again for the first time after the divorce, when she becomes attracted to Velutha. As in the preceding chapters, Roy makes allusions to the events surrounding Sophie Mol s death and the reason Estha stopped talking. Still she does not reveal these things, keeping them as hidden for the reader as they are for the characters. Roy suggests that if life is unpredictable and nonlinear, then a story about life should be equally so.

Sophie Mol s welcome wagon is, like the hotel in Cochin, an example of an attempt at cultural diplomacy that results in awkwardness and falseness. Instead of treating Sophie like one of its own, the family puts on airs to entertain and impress her as though the family's pride depends upon her approval. Instead of wanting Sophie and Margaret to be fascinated with their culture, they create a sort of hybrid culture involving Western violin music and a Westernized iced cake. When the truly Indian the dark, bare-bodied Velutha and Kochu Maria s kissing custom invades the scene, Ammu cannot stand it. She retreats to the house and tells Rahel not to play with Velutha so much. Although the hybrid cultural elements are in a sense a phony put-on, there is safety within it, because Ammu does not have to explain herself or her actions, but can pretend that her purpose is to be a good hostess and show a small, grieving child a good time.

The theme of mutability pervades these chapters as Roy develops the refrain, Things can change in a day. Ammu becomes attracted to Velutha in a day, and she goes from living to dead in a day. As we know, Sophie Mol also goes from living to dead in a day. Everyone is alive one day and dead the next. In keeping with her pattern, Roy makes sure to include the world of "Small Things" in developing the theme of mutability. Rahel expresses her anger at Ammu and her jealousy towards Sophie Mol by squashing ants. Although we witness Rahel's violence only from the human perspective, we can imagine the colony of ants as representing the crowd of people celebrating Sophie Mol's arrival. Rahel has a power over them that she wishes she had over the adults in her world. If we extrapolate from this focus on the influence of "Small Things," we can conclude that the people in Ayemenem are just as fragile and vulnerable to sudden change or sudden death as the ants.

Summary and Analysis of Chapters 10-12

Chapter 10 - The River in the Boat

While the crowd celebrates Sophie Mol s arrival, Estha is by himself in the pickle factory. He stirs the illegal banana jam while thinking his Two Thoughts, to which Roy has previously alluded. The first is that Anything can happen to anyone, and the second is that It s best to be prepared. Estha is becoming lost in macabre thoughts, including his continuing fear of the Orangedrink Lemondrink man, when Rahel barges into the factory and interrupts him. Estha tells Rahel that he is going to visit the History House, where no one ever goes. The last person there was Vellya Paapen, who said that it was haunted by the ghost of Kari Saipu.

There in the factory, Rahel and Estha 'pickle, seal, and put away' a secret plan to visit the History House together. Rahel meets Estha on the riverbank. (For the first time, Roy states directly that Ammu and Velutha will have an affair.) When Estha and Rahel try to launch the boat, they sink into the river with it. They wash the boat and bring it ashore, then plant a Communist flag in the ground. They approach Velutha s hut, where his crippled brother, Kuttappen, is repeating obscenities. The twins bring him the boat and he gives them advice about how to fix it. He also warns them that the river isn t always what she pretends to be.

Velutha arrives. The thought of Ammu s children being in his home excites him in a new way, but he banishes the thought guiltily. He promises to fix the boat for them. Having seen the Communist flag, Velutha tells Kuttappen he knows the twins saw him marching. Again he must try to suppress his growing attraction to Ammu.

Chapter 11 - The God of Small Things

Ammu dreams of wanting a one-armed man to make love to her. In the dream, the presence of others prevents this from happening. Ammu and the one-armed man swim together in a treacherous sea, not touching. The twins watch Ammu nap, thinking she is having a nightmare. They wake her up gently. Ammu tells them that she was having a good dream. Ammu senses that the children have been to see Veluth, so she scolds them. Then she lets them fondle the stretch marks on her belly from when she was pregnant with them. When she has had enough, she goes into the bathroom and examines her body in the mirror. She weeps for herself, the twins, and the God of Small Things.

From the adult Rahel s perspective, later, Rahel thinks about the family s dissolution. The scene switches back to Rahel watching fondly as Estha bathes silently in the moonlight.

Chapter 12 - Kochu Thomban

Rahel enters a temple, where she approaches the sleeping elephant, Kochu Thomban. Rahel watches traditional kathkali dancers act out a play. The novel's narrator explains (as has already been suggested) that the traditional, treasured art of kathkali has been cheapened since it was assimilated into the business of entertaining tourists. The kathkali dancer in the modern world hawks the only thing he owns. The stories that his body can tell. He becomes a Regional Flavor. Rahel watches as the dancers reenact the story of Karna, a man born in poverty who dies at the hands of his own brother. It is a very violent story about family and betrayal. She is swept up in the performance when she senses Estha s arrival in the temple.

The performance goes on all through the night. Though the twins sit separately, they are bound together by the story and the way it makes them think of their own family. They are brought out of their trance only by the elephant s cracking open of the coconut that Rahel brought for it. Roy writes: The Kathkali Men took off their makeup and went home to beat their wives. Even Kunti, the soft one with breasts.

We learn that it was Comrade Pillai who introduced Estha and Rahel to kathkali, along with his own son, Lenin. At that moment, Comrade Pillai walks into the temple. He says, You are here! So still you are interested in your Indian culture? Goodgood. Very good. The twins say nothing and walk home in silence.

Analysis

These chapters use fantasies to probe the sex-violence connection that Roy established early on. In the pickle factory, Estha dwells on his fear of the Orangedrink Lemondrink man. Like the banana jam he stirs, the fact of his molestation is both illicit and skillfully hidden away. The sexual violence becomes a Small Thing in Estha s life, relegated to private thoughts in private places. Estha s fantasies are, therefore, as anxious and sad as the feelings he carries with him silently.

Ammu s dream about the one-armed man is both sexual and violent. Although she and her dream lover never touch, it is as though they are making love through their deep connection to one another. This sex is connected to violence in several ways. First, the dream actualized (Ammu's and Velutha s affair) leads to Velutha s death. There is violence implicit in the fact that Ammu s dream lover has only one arm, since he must have lost the other. Because of his disability, he perhaps can only do one thing to or for her at a time. The dream lover s disability represents the fact that Velutha can be only one thing to Ammu, a secret lover. The fantasy played out by the kathkali dancers in the temple also fuses sex and violence. The story itself is macabre, but it has a certain beauty, like the blood spilling poetically from the fallen painter s skull in chapter 1. As soon as the play ends, all beauty disappears and the violence is pure; the actors go home to beat their wives. In Roy s world, fantasy is safer than reality, but always infiltrated by it. Even pleasant dreams like Ammu s are full of implicit violence, danger, and grief. Roy draws our attention to the fact that even while the twins were fetuses suspended in Ammu s belly, they caused her a type of violence, kicking her and leaving stretch marks.

The kathkali dancers and Comrade Pillai are examples of the strange cultural fusion we saw in Sophie Mol s welcome party. The dancers practice a traditional and very nuanced cultural art, but they are forced to cheapen it by making it attractive to tourists; spaces like the temple are the only ones where the kathkali dancers can really act in their element, performing stories as they are intended. Comrade Pillai is a paradox in himself. He is pleased that the twins are still interested in their native culture and visiting the temple, but he also invests himself almost wholly in the Communist cause, one very much outside his culture's political, social, and economic caste system.

Summary and Analysis of Chapters 13-15

Chapter 13 - The Pessimist and the Optimist

Sophie Mol awakens in the guest room of the Ayemenem house. For the first time, her first thought is not of her deceased father. She watches her mother sleep and looks at her divorced parents framed wedding picture.

We turn to the story of Chacko and Margaret Kochamma. They met in Oxford, England, where he was a student on a Rhodes Scholarship and she was working as a waitress, saving up for teacher training. She told him a joke about the Man with Twin Sons, Pete the Optimist and Stuart and Pessimist. On their birthday, the father gave Stuart expensive gifts, which he did not like. He filled Pete s room with horse dung. When he went into Pete s room he was met by frantic shoveling, and Pete said: If there s so much shit around, there has to be a pony somewhere. Margaret Kochamma and Chacko shared a laughing fit. After that, they became lovers. Chacko entranced Margaret with his passionate eccentricity. Chacko loved Margaret s independence. Yet once they were married, their love began to dissolve. Chacko became fat, and Margaret could no longer stand his sloppiness at home and in his appearance. They moved from small apartment to small apartment. Just when Margaret found out she was pregnant, she met Joe and fell in love with him out of pure attraction mingled with desperation. When Sophie was born, Margaret asked Chacko for a divorce. Chacko returned to India while Margaret stayed in England. At Mammachi s house, Chacko s eccentricity and sloppiness embarrassed guests. Still, Mammachi adored her son, especially since he had defended her against Pappachi.

Back in England, Margaret was very happy with Joe and wrote Chacko letters telling him about her life and Sophie s life. The former husband and wife developed a friendship via writing. Joe s accidental death devastated Margaret and Sophie, so when Chacko invited them to India, they gladly accepted.

Back in the present, Margaret can never get the image of her daughter s corpse out of her mind. She cannot forgive herself for leaving Sophie in Ayemenem while she and Chacko went to Cochin to confirm her and her daughter s plane tickets.

A new sub-chapter begins. We finally hear the story of Sophie Mol s death. The morning Sophie s body was found floating in the river, she and the twins had not shown up for breakfast. As Ammu heard the news, she suddenly remembered what happened the night before. While locked in her room, she had shrieked at the twins: If it wasn t for you I wouldn t be here! None of this would have happened! I wouldn t be here! I would have been free! I should have dumped you in an orphanage the day you were born! *You re* the millstones round my neck!

The previous afternoon, it was raining nonstop, and Vellya Paapen arrived at the house drunk. When Mammachi finally let him in, he began to blabber about how grateful he was to her family. Then he told Mammachi that Ammu and Velutha, her daughter and his son, were having an affair. Mammachi shouted so loudly that she could not hear what she was saying. She pushed Vellya Paapen down the stairs. He offered to kill Velutha with his bare hands. Baby Kochamma felt vindicated when she heard the news, because she had always been jealous of Ammu. Mammachi, Baby Kochamma, and Kochu Maria locked Ammu up in her room and sent for Velutha.

The narrative shifts to a fisherman finding Sophie Mol s body in the river. Then it shifts to the police station, where Baby Kochamma recounted the discovery of Ammu and Velutha s affair to an officer. Equally to salvage the family s pride and to indulge her own love of melodrama, she said that Velutha had raped Ammu and made him out to be an ungrateful criminal. (We recall that later, Ammu tried to set the record straight to no avail.)

Back at the house, Margaret Kochamma saw Sophie s corpse for the first time. She was so traumatized that she could not remember the next few days. Margaret was furious at the twins for having survived. She instinctively knew that it was all Estha s idea to go out on the water, and before leaving India she sought him out and slapped him without knowing what she was doing. Years later she wrote an apology letter, but only the adult Rahel was there to claim it. Margaret never knew that Velutha had been arrested. In the last part of this sub-chapter, Roy names Velutha The God of Loss and The God of Small Things, a being who left no footprints in sand, no ripples in water, no image in mirrors.

A new sub-chapter begins. We return to Sophie Mol, who is waking up and looking at her parents wedding picture. After watching Chacko leave, she sets off with presents for Estha and Rahel. We learn that Sophie Mol became a Memory, while The Loss of Sophie Mol grew robust and alive. Like a fruit in season. Every season.

Chapter 14- Work is Struggle

After Sophie watches him leave the house, Chacko pays a visit to Comrade Pillai s house. Over the latter s doorway hangs a proclamation: Work is struggle. Struggle is work. Comrade Pillai is out, so Chacko waits uncomfortably with the former's mother, his wife Kalyani, son Lenin, and niece Latha. Comrade Pillai arrives. He insists on speaking to Chacko in English. Chacko wants him to approve a new label for the factory s new product, Synthetic Cooking Vinegar. They discuss Velutha. Comrade Pillai tells Chacko that Velutha will cause him trouble because he is a Paravan. Chacko defends Velutha.

Eventually, Paradise Pickles & Preserves folded. Comrade Pillai was the last person to see Velutha before The last betrayal that sent [him] across the river, swimming against the current, in the dark and rain, well in time for his blind date with history.

Another new sub-chapter begins. Mammachi summons Velutha to her house. As soon as he arrives, she lays into him with yelling and insults. She banishes him from her property and says that if she ever finds him there, she will have him killed. She spits in his face. Velutha says simply, We ll see about that, before leaving. Sapped and revolted, he heads straight to Comrade Pillai s house. He asks for the Party s help, but Comrade Pillai refuses and sends him away. After he shuts the door on Velutha, Comrade Pillai remarks that Velutha is wearing red nail polish, which the children painted on earlier. Velutha feels as though he has no control over his body or actions--as though he is a slave to history and destiny.

Chapter 15 - The Crossing

It is after midnight. Velutha strips naked and swims across the river to the History House, completely undetected and undetectable. He is sad and beautiful in the moonlight as he moves deliberately but unconsciously. Again Roy refers to him as The God of Loss and The God of Small Things.

Analysis

We finally hear the story of the events surrounding Sophie Mol s death, which have remained tantalizing allusions throughout the novel. Using the terms Roy has established, the Small Things begin to creep out into the world of Big Things and wreak social havoc. This process is symbolized by Vellya Paapen s coming to Mammachi s house. Although the two families have a generations-long understanding, suddenly instead of being welcome, Vellya Paapen is an intruder from the riverbank world of Small Things and the correspondingly unattractive history. Mammachi wants to squash him like one of Rahel s ants; for the first time in many years, she wields her power over him in a destructive way. Once power is in the hands of the furious Mammachi and the petty Baby Kochamma, the Small Things are no longer safe. Without realizing what she is doing, Ammu turns to the destructive cause by screaming her insult at the twins. Instinctively, they retreat to the riverbank, to the world of Small Things. The twins would rather dwell in the shadows with the truth than in the comfort of the Ayemenem House with lies and pretentiousness.

Velutha echoes his father s intrusion into the world of Big Things when he arrives at Comrade Pillai s door. The latter does not want to acknowledge him as a human being worthy of his assistance, even though he is a card-carrying Communist Party member. Like Mammachi and Baby Kochamma, Comrade Pillai will do whatever it takes even mistreating another human being in order to maintain their honor and prevent themselves from slipping into the world of notoriety and Small Things. Society, the world of Big Things, instinctively protects itself when presented with reality.

Because Estha and Rahel are lovers of the truth, unlike their families, Sophie s death stays with them right up until we meet them as adults, as present as the day it happened. Roy writes, The Loss of Sophie Mol grew robust and alive. Like a fruit in season. Every season. If we think back to the opening of the novel, we can see how the ripeness of Sophie s death connects to the atmosphere of Ayemenem. Her death is not only a central trauma for the twins, but it also occurs amidst a culmination of the overly lush, overly sensuous nature that overruns Ayemenem in the warm months. Sophie s death may not be a "Big Thing" but may be the ultimate Small Thing, hidden in shadows in the river and on the riverbank, locked away in the ugly realm of history for being too scandalous, too horrifyingly delicious.

In the Harper Perennial edition of the novel, the sub-chapters are separated by small graphics of fish. When Sophie s body is pulled from the river, her eyelids are partially eaten away by fish she has succumbed once and for all to the world of Small Things. These fish graphics appear as though in defiance of the social outrage surrounding Sophie s death, forcing us to confront physical images of a Small Thing even as the family tries to suppress that world of truth, what really happened. There are aspects of reality that cannot be changed by socially deconstructing them out of existence.

In these chapters, Roy begins to refer to Velutha as The God of Small Things. Suddenly, he takes on a much greater importance, since now he is not only a divine being but the title character of the story. Until this time there has been no main character, except perhaps the twins as a leading duo. Now, however, Roy asserts that the story is really Velutha s. He is The God of Loss, who [leaves] no footprints in sand, no ripples in water, no image in mirrors. He is the bastion of the world of sacred, "untouchable" secrets, whispers, and overlooked pieces of reality. In appropriate fashion, until Roy names Velutha, we are unaware that his role in the novel is so central it seems like a subplot. But this is appropriate to his quiet, barely detectable nature. He moves through and eventually leaves the world quietly and without incident.

Summary and Analysis of Chapters 16-18

Chapter 16 - A Few Hours Later

We find Estha, Rahel, and Sophie setting out on the river in their boat. Sophie has convinced the twins that she must run away with them to make the adults even more upset. They row for a little while and then bump into a log and capsize. Rahel and Estha emerge on the shore without Sophie. After searching for her for hours, they finally collapse on the veranda of the History House. They do not see Velutha sleeping in the shadows.

Chapter 17 - Cochin Harbor Terminus

Having ironed his and Rahel s clothes, the adult Estha sits in his bed in the dark. Kochu Maria sleeps. Baby Kochamma writes in her diary. She begins every entry in it with I love you I love you, thinking of Father Mulligan. They stayed in touch until his death a few years earlier, before which he had left the church to become a follower of Vishnu. Although he rejected her romantically in life, after his death Baby Kochamma developed an imaginary, loving relationship with him through her diary. The twins sit quietly on one bed. Estha remembers the last time he saw Ammu before he left for Assam. We learn that Velutha was arrested after Sophie Mol s death and was charged with kidnapping and murder. After that, Comrade Pillai led a Communist siege of the pickle factory, claiming that Velutha was being persecuted for his party affiliation.

Chapter 18 - The History House

Back on the day of Sophie Mol s death, policemen cross the river looking for clues. They trudge amidst small creatures and the beauty of nature. They come upon the History House, on which veranda Estha, Rahel and Velutha are sleeping. They beat Velutha savagely, to the children s horror. The policemen have no sense of Velutha as a fellow human being, because he is an Untouchable. The twins learn two new lessons, the first that Blood barely shows on a Black Man, and the second that It smells though, sicksweet, like roses on a breeze. Even though Velutha is beaten so badly that he cannot move, the policemen handcuff him and drag him off. They feel good about saving the twins from this Untouchable, and they steal the toys lying around the veranda for their own children.

Analysis

After so many chapters building up to the actual telling of Sophie Mol s death, the incident is extremely quick. Sophie drowns in a mere instant and by accident. All the scandal surrounding her murder has to do more with other people s social conflicts than with her death. For the twins, it is not even their role in Sophie s death that haunts them throughout their lives, but the fact that surrounding it were Ammu s renunciation of them and Velutha s murder. For Estha and Rahel, Sophie Mol s death really signifies the day on which they lost both their mother and father figures.

In the previous three chapters, the world of Small Things invaded the world of Big Things when Vellya Paapen and Velutha visited Mammachi s and Comrade Pillai s houses, respectively. Now the world of Big Things not only invades but demolishes the world of Small Things. The policemen are the ultimate symbol of the world of Big Things. They are sanctioned by society to destroy with hard boots and weapons and loud voices, putting them immediately at odds with the lively, quiet lushness of Small Things. It is especially clear that the policemen and Velutha come from a different world when they beat him nearly to death; as the God of Small Things, he is seen as a Small Thing himself, unimportant and non-human. When the children witness their friend and guardian being abused, they see their haven crumbling before them. Hours before, they had fled into that haven, away from Ammu s accusations. Now there is nowhere safe for them; perhaps this is why even as adults, they cannot seem to stay in one place. Perhaps this is also why they are drawn back to Ayemenem, to reclaim the world of Small Things and come to terms with their painful secrets now that enough time has passed and enough people have passed away.

Summary and Analysis of Chapters 19-21

Chapter 19 - Saving Ammu

At the police station, Inspector Thomas Mathew gives Estha and Rahel some Cokes. He sends for Baby Kochamma, whom he tells that Velutha will probably not live through the night. He then tells her that the children say they went with Velutha of their own volition and that Sophie drowned accidentally; therefore the police are about to have an innocent man s death on their hands. If someone does not substantiate Baby Kochamma s claim that Velutha is a criminal in this case, she will be charged with filing a false account. Alone with the twins, Baby Kochamma tells them they have murdered Sophie. She terrorizes the children with thoughts of being alone in jail for the rest of their lives in order to pressure them into substantiating her claim. She gives them the option of saving Ammu or sending her to jail. The children, of course, choose to save her.

Inspector Thomas Mathew takes Estha in to identify Velutha. He is naked and near death. Roy tells us that blood spilled from his skull like a secret. Estha does as Baby Kochamma told him and identifies Velutha as the man who abducted the children. All he knows is that he answers yes to the policeman s question. Velutha dies that night. In fear of her dishonesty being exposed, Baby Kochamma coerces Chacko into forcefully evicting Ammu from the house and sending Estha away to live with Babu.

Chapter 20 - The Madras Mail

Estha sits on the train carrying him away from Ayemenem. The woman sitting next to him offers him sweets and makes him an example for her children since he speaks such good English. We learn that only as adults do the children understand Ammu s role in Velutha s death. The twins and Ammu had loved [Velutha] to death. Estha himself bears the weight of having killed Ammu, since out of fear he said he would never see her again. As we know, both the twins bear the weight of Sophie s death well into adulthood. As Estha s train pulls out of the station, Rahel doubles over and screams as though in terrible pain.

A new sub-chapter begins. We are back in the present. The adult Rahel calls Estha by his fond childhood name, Esthapappychachen Kuttappen Peter Mon. He traces her mouth with his fingers, and then they lie holding each other on the bed. Then the twins make love. Although there is very little that anyone could say to clarify what happened, it is sure that they act more out of hideous grief than anything else. Rahel remembers that Ammu tucked her into bed on the night of Sophie Mol s arrival. As Ammu left the room, she longed for him. Ached for him with the whole of her body.

Chapter 21 - The Cost of Living

After everyone is asleep, Ammu listens to her radio on the veranda. She runs to the riverbank sobbing, hoping that Velutha will meet her there. He does not come; he is floating in the river, stargazing. He too is disappointed, having been so sure that Ammu would meet him on this night. Suddenly he sees her and swims over to where she sits. They embrace, and Ammu kisses him. They make love there on the riverbank. The experience is profound and somehow removed from time, even though it is the catalyst for the events leading up to Velutha s own violent death. During all of their clandestine meetings after that, Ammu and Velutha focus on the Small Things, small and present pleasures, insects, the details of one another s bodies. In particular, they keep watch over a spider, which Velutha names Lord Rubbish. They leave the Big Things, the realities of daily life, behind. Sadly, even Lord Rubbish lives longer than Velutha. When Ammu and Velutha part at the end of each night, they say simply: Tomorrow? Tomorrow. After they make love on the night of Sophie Mol s arrival, Ammu turns back to repeat Tomorrow one more time before heading back to the house.

Analysis

In the final three chapters, Baby Kochamma emerges as a villain. In her old age she seems mundane and harmless, but in fact she is behind much of the family s scandal. Her nervousness at the twins return to Ayemenem is not unsubstantiated; after all, she is the one who pressured Estha into identifying Velutha as guilty, she who made Ammu and Estha leave Ayemenem. Baby Kochamma sees herself as the ultimate protector of the Big Things, most importantly the family s honor. Finding her own life uninteresting, she meddles with others lives in order to make sure that she looks reputable.

Roy s use of the grotesque crescendos in the final three chapters as Velutha is beaten by the police and left to suffer a somewhat slow and agonizing death. At Sophie Mol s funeral, Rahel imagines blood spilling from the ceiling-painter s skull like a secret. Hers is a violent but somehow beautiful image of death. Roy uses the exact same phrase, blood spilling from his skull like a secret, to describe Velutha as Estha sees him, on the brink of death. Although Velutha is The God of Small Things, he is not invincible; he dies like something small, crushed and beaten like an insect. Yet his death is also somehow romantic and beautiful like the ceiling-painter s; he dies as a result of taking a risk for his passion (for Ammu as opposed to painting ceilings). Despite his body s crumpled, oozing condition when he dies, Velutha's nails are still painted red (the twins' handiwork). Even in a most decrepit state and near death, the best, most human part of Velutha still exists. He has always been the type of person who puts children and their desires, however trivial or silly, first.

The twins incest also falls under the categories of the grotesque and of Small Things. It is an act that must be hidden away, if not by the river like Ammu's and Velutha s affair, then in the silence behind closed doors. The twins make love not out of passion but hideous grief." Estha is so traumatized that he cannot communicate through words, so the twins use their bodies to express their deepest sorrows--for the deaths of Ammu, Velutha, and Sophie.

Finally the Freudian undercurrent of the novel is revealed. When distressing memories are repressed, they can begin to take over one's personality until they become central even as they are ignored. Eventually, these hidden things begin to reveal themselves, sometimes in small ways as in a dream, sometimes in big ways as in this consummatory incest.

Roy leaves us with a hopeful view of life despite the horrors that are exposed in the final chapters. The last chapter is entitled The Cost of Living, which can be paraphrased as Death. The author suggests that like Homer's Achilles, one can either live well at the risk of dying early, or live a long life that is unfulfilled. Baby Kochamma never got her torrid love affair with Father Mulligan, so she lives vicariously through her diary and television. But Ammu and Velutha live a most vibrant, rich life together in secret before dying prematurely. Instead of being so concerned with the Big Things that they are trapped in unhappiness, they relish the Small Things and each other, eternally hopeful for Tomorrow.

Suggested Essay Questions

1. In The God of Small Things, various "Big Things" and "Small Things" are constantly at odds. Define "Big Things" and "Small Things" in your own terms, and then determine whether one class of things or the other becomes ascendant by the end. Or are they always equal and opposite sets of things?

2. Roy refers to Velutha as both "The God of Small Things" and "The God of Loss." Using specific examples from the text, explain what about Velutha makes these titles appropriate or inappropriate.

3. Compare Ammu's and Velutha's secret sexual relationship to Rahel's and Estha's incestuous tryst. Is one or the other more forbidden? How do they express the psychology of the various characters involved?

4. Examine Roy's use of "Small Things" and the 'small perspective' throughout the novel. Why does she insist on focusing on what is small? Are things small by nature or by convention? Consider the novel's epigraph in this context.

5. Explore Paradise Pickles & Preserves as a symbol for the forbidden and hidden in The God of Small Things. How does the process of pickling serve as a metaphor for the way the family handles its 'skeletons in the closet'?

6. How does Roy use the idea of loyalty in the novel? Which characters are loyal and which are disloyal? Some characters to consider: Comrade Pillai, Baby Kochamma, Velutha, Ammu, Estha.

7. Explain how violence and sex are connected throughout the novel. In Roy's world, can one exist without the other, or are they necessarily connected? What sort of outlook does this create?

8. Examine Roy's use of the grotesque in the story's events as well as the characters' fantasies. Is any of the violence Roy uses gratuitous? If so, how? If not, why is so much violence necessary in the novel?

9. Consider Roy's literary style. How does her use of perspective, time, fantasy, refrain, and any other element you wish to discuss affect the way we perceive the story?

10. Examine Roy's use of setting in the novel. How do her choices serve to highlight a connection or disconnection between the worlds of "Big Things" and "Small Things"? Some locations to consider: The river and riverbank, Ayemenem as a whole, Cochin, the History House, the Ayemenem House, the hotel, the movie theater, Ammu's room, the police station.

11. Does The God of Small Things have one definite protagonist? If so, who is it and why? If not, why does the novel need no single protagonist?

12. Contrast one of the following sets of characters, using specific examples from the text: Velutha and Estha, Ammu and Rahel, Sophie and Rahel, Baby Kochamma and Mammachi, Chacko and Comrade Pillai. What makes the comparison worth noting? Do not compare characters unless you can argue why the comparison is worthwhile.

13. Which affects Estha's and Rahel's relationship more, their shared experience, or their instinctive, biological connection from birth? Make sure

you can substantiate your claim with regard to episodes such as their incest, the incident with the Orangedrink Lemondrink man, Sophie Mol's death, and the scene at the police station with Baby Kochamma.

Kerala, India

Kerala is a state at the southwestern tip of India, meeting the Arabian Sea on the west and the Ghat mountains on the east. The state s tourism board coined its official slogan God s Own Country. Like many Indian states, Kerala has its own creation myth. As the legend goes, a wise warrior named Parsurama created Kerala in an attempt to avenge his father s murder. He wreaked havoc on the clan of the Kshatriya king who killed his father, but afterwards was stricken with terrible remorse. After he repented, Varuna, the god of the sea, promised him a portion of land extending as far into the ocean as he could throw his axe. Parsurama did so, and the land that arose from the water became the territory of Kerala.

In more modern history, Kerala achieved statehood in 1956 after existing as part of the Travancore-Cochin region since India s independence in 1947. Kerala's official language is Malayalam, although it is not uncommon for inhabitants to be familiar with several other languages from neighboring territories.

Hindus, Christians, and Muslims are the primary religious groups occupying Kerala in addition to many minor ones. The state's religious diversity is a testament to the many groups that have inhabited the land throughout history, and this is one reason Roy's novel takes place here. Inhabitants have included Portuguese, Dutch, British, rulers from all over India, and religious groups escaping persecution in their own countries.

Kerala is lauded for its outstanding progress in the areas of cleanliness, education, and quality of life. The tourism board of Kerala boasts that it is not only India s cleanest state but also has a literacy rate above ninety percent and the highest physical quality of life in India.

Kerala has a rich cultural heritage that includes many art forms. Perhaps the most recognizable of these is the traditional dance-storytelling art of Kathakali. The form originated in the seventeenth century, and it has become a hallmark of the region ever since. Over the course of several hours, trained and exquisitely costumed actors play out traditional stories while singing, dancing, and using hand gestures known as mudras. There are at least seven other dance and dramatic forms native to Kerala, including the original acting style of Koodiyattom. During festivals, elephant pageants are requisite, complete with costumes for humans and animals, music, and fireworks displays.

Also central to the culture of Kerala is the tradition of Malayalam literature, which is at least 1,000 years old. Some of the most notable works of Malayalam literature are the *Ramacharitam*, the first of many poetry-based Malayalam versions of the *Ramayana*, as well as the *Attakkatha*, a genre of poetry used as the libretto for Kathakali performances. Other works are influenced by or reacting to the genres of British or Western literature in more recent times, plus literary criticism and an essay tradition.

Author of ClassicNote and Sources

Tania Asnes, author of ClassicNote. Completed on July 27, 2006, copyright held by GradeSaver.

Updated and revised Adam Kissel September 30, 2006. Copyright held by GradeSaver.

Jones, Clifford, and Betty True. Kathakali: An Introduction to the Dance-drama of Kerala. San Francisco: American Society for Eastern Arts, 1970.

Roy, Arundhati. The God of Small Things. New York: Harper Perennial, 1997.

Pushpanath, Salim. The Magic of Kerala. Kottayam: Dee Bee Info Publications, 2004.

"Kerala Pictures." 2006-07-19. <http://www.keralapictures.com>.

"Government of Kerala." 2006-07-21. <http://www.kerala.gov.in>.

K. Ayyappapanicker. "Malayalam Literature." 2006-07-25. <http://www.cs.princeton.edu/~mp/malayalam/copy/prdkerala.org/mallitrature.htm>.

Arundhati Roy. "The Most Cowardly War in History." Truthout.org. 2006-07-15. <http://www.truthout.org/docs_2005/062505Y.shtml>.

Seby Varghese Thokkadam. "Arundhati Roy: A Life Full of Beginnings and No Ends." 2006-07-15. <http://www.chitram.org/mallu/ar.htm>.

Vir Sanghvi. "The Rediff Special: Interview with Arundhati Roy." Rediff on the Net. 2006-07-15. <http://www.rediff.com/news/apr/05roy.htm>.

"Arundhati Roy." Voices from the Gaps. 2006-07-27. <http://voices.cla.umn.edu/vg/Bios/entries/roy_arundhati.html>.

Essay: Growth, Confusion, and the Loss of Innocence: The Differing Roles of Childlike Narration in Roy's The God of Small Things and Faulkner's The Sound and the Fury

by Jane Park
November 18, 2002

One, a story about culture, class, family, and love laws, follows the lives of a pair of twins in Kerala, India as they learn one fateful December day how drastically "Things Can Change in a Day." The other, a story about suicide and incestual desire, tells of the fall of the Compson family from four different perspectives. How can these two seemingly different novels - The Sound and the Fury by William Faulkner and The God of Small Things by Arundhati Roy - possibly be related? In both novels, the reader finds himself reading a childlike account of the events that come to pass through the course of the novels. The lack of insight, limited use of modifiers, and simplistic sentence structure of Benjy's section and the phonetic spelling, whimsical adjectives, and interspersed lines of children's songs of The God of Small Things both serve to present the reader with childlike descriptions of the stories. However, they differ not only in the level of insight reached by each of the narrators by the conclusion of the novels, but also in the purpose of the childlike descriptions. In contrast to Benjy's childlike narration that creates a sense of confusion within the reader that parallels his confusion, the childlike quality of Roy's narration sophisticatedly creates a lightheartedness that starkly contrasts against the heavy tone and serious nature of the material, thus representing the gap between innocence and corruption.

While Roy and Faulkner both present the reader with childlike renditions of the events, they approach and accomplish this task through differing methods. Faulkner chooses to tell the section "April Seventh, 1928" from the viewpoint of a mentally-challenged thirty-three-year-old-man. He writes simplistically: "Luster had some spools and he and Quentin fought and Quentin had the spools. Luster cried and Frony came and gave Luster a tin can to play with, and then I had the spools and Quentin fought me and I cried" (Faulkner 19). Within the span of two sentences, Benjy repeats the word spools three times, the verb fought two times, and the verb cried twice. There is no variation; he simply reuses the same word repeatedly when there are a plethora of synonyms that could easily have been substituted in its place. In addition, he only provides the reader with the bare essential facts necessary to formulate an understanding of the event. He gives the subject and the verb, but there are no adverbs and only a few adjectives. What color are the spools? What are they made of? These questions could easily be answered with the addition of a few adjectives, but adjectives are scarce in Benjy's section. The limited vocabulary, virtual absence of modifiers, and simplistic sentence structure of Benjy categorizes his writing style as being characteristic of a child, for it lacks the sophistication usually associated with the more mature writing of an adult. Consisting mostly of nouns and verbs, his account of the events that pass does not extend beyond the mere reporting of the actions he witnesses and experiences. The lack of proper punctuation serves to portray his narration as a report. Luster asks Benjy: "Ain't you going to help me find that quarter so I can go to the show tonight" (Faulkner 3). While the proper punctuation here should be a question mark, the end of the statement is punctuated with a period; this substitution flattens the speech so that there is no evidence of voice inflection or emotion. This flattening of speech shows that Benjy cannot distinguish between a question and normal speech - it is all the same to him. Thus, he is only able to report what he hears. Similarly, although he describes what he sees, he does not possess the capability to interpret the actions. For example, the novel opens with a scene in which the children are playing. Benjy describes: "Then they put the flag back and they went to the table and he hit and the other hit" (Faulkner 3). Although the word hit is a transitive verb, he uses it intransitively. Never does he mention what "they" are hitting - the direct object - or what the game is. It is only when Luster says "'Here, caddie'" does the reader know that "they" are playing golf (Faulkner 3). Because of Faulkner's decision to tell the story from the viewpoint of a mentally-challenged individual, the reader experiences the events as if he were looking through the eyes of a child.

In contrast to Faulkner's choice of simplicity, Roy incorporates phonetic spelling, whimsical adjectives, and interspersed lines of song into the narration to give it a childlike quality. Phrases such as "Their Prer NUN sea ayshun was perfect" and "cheerful chop-chop-chopping" cue the reader that the narrator is a child (Roy 147, 121). But it is interesting that the childlike quality conveys the message more effectively than if it had been absent. For example, in "Their Prer NUN sea ayshun was perfect," the phonetic spelling of the word pronunciation emphasizes the pronunciation of the word, for it is only by saying "Prer NUN sea ayshun" aloud that the reader is able to realize that the broken group of syllables refers to the word pronunciation. By the time the reader finishes reading the word aloud, she has been forced to pause from the normal act of reading and finds herself engaged in a study of pronunciation of the word pronunciation, much like the manner in which they study pronunciation. Thus, the form in which the word is presented to the reader reinforces the content. And in "cheerful chop-chop-chopping," the lengthening of the word chopping into "chop-chop-chopping" creates a sing-song quality that portrays the act of chopping as being cheerful, thus reiterating the adjective that precedes it; in other words, the style reinforces the content. Roy also uses whimsical adjectives as well. When the narrator describes a tune that Mammachi plays on her violin, she describes it as "A cloying, chocolate melody. Stickysweet, and meltybrown. Chocolate waves on a chocolate shore" (Roy 174). This metaphor may seem like nonsense at first, for what can chocolate possibly have in common with a melody? But it is not nonsensical, for both are rich; one is rich in taste while the other is rich in sound. Furthermore, it is fitting to describe the sound as a chocolate "wave" not only because sound resonates when the perfect pitch is attained, but also because sounds physically are waves that travel through the air. And to further elaborate upon the metaphor, as chocolate melts in one's mouth, one can "melt" into the music as one relaxes and surrenders oneself to the swirling melodies that envelop its listeners. In addition, the interspersed lines of children's songs throughout the work contribute to the childlike quality of the writing. As Rahel climbs up the stairs with Baby Kochamma, she sings the song "Popeye the Sailorman" and fills in "Dum Dums" whenever there are pauses. The interspersed lines of children's songs, cheerful alliteration, and phonetic spelling that can be found throughout the narration all contribute to the formation of a playful, lighthearted, relaxed tone that portrays the innocence of childhood.

However, while both narrations are childlike in their own manner, the childlike qualities serve different purposes in each novel. Faulkner's decision to write Benjy's section in the form of stream of consciousness and the lack of transitions between the rapid switching of scenes creates a sense of confusion within the reader. As the reader tackles the first page of the novel, he encounters the following passage: "'Can't you never crawl through here without snagging on that nail.' Caddy uncaught me and we crawled through" (Faulkner 3). The two statements are obviously connected, for both are about Benjy being snagged on a nail, but the characters have changed. Where is Luster, and where does Caddy come from? The change in characters is the only clue that there has been a switching of scenes. That both scenes address the common topic of Benjy being snagged on a nail makes it difficult to notice that one sentence belongs to the narration of one scene while the other is related to an entirely different one - the switching of scenes is cleverly disguised. In reality, the first sentence takes place in the present, but the second takes place on December 25th, a day when Caddy and Benjy delivered a letter to Mrs. Patterson. Thus, the free association among the past and present experiences that Benjy makes confuses the reader so that the reader can properly focalize through the narrator by identifying with Benjy's confusion. Benjy's retardation prevents him from perceiving his surroundings as normal people do. Benjy blurs the boundaries between present reality and the past, so it is only fitting that the reader has difficulty distinguishing between the past and present, as Benjy does. Constantly throughout the novel, he lacks an awareness of his surroundings and of himself. Repeatedly, he doesn't realize that its cold and has to have others tell him to put his hands in his pockets. The reader finds out about Benjy from cues of those around him. For example, through the phrase "What are you moaning about, Luster said," the reader finds out that Benjy has been moaning (Faulkner 5). The reader is not provided with any information that Benjy himself does not have; she learns as Benjy learns. Since Benjy's understanding of the events around him is minimal, the reader is provided merely with disordered fragments of information with which he has to struggle to piece together to form an understanding of the situation. Thus, the writing style of Benjy's section creates confusion within the reader that parallel's Benjy's confusion that results from his diminished mental abilities.

Unlike Faulkner, Roy uses the childlike narration not to parallel a particular character, but to create a stark contrast between the playful lightheartedness of the tone and the seriousness of the material under discussion. The day that the Orangedrink Lemondrink Man molests Estha, Estha has difficulty sleeping at night because he feels nauseous. Roy describes: "Estha Alone walked wearily to the bathroom. He vomited a clear, bitter, lemony, sparkly, fizzy liquid. The acrid aftertaste of a Little Man's first encounter with Fear. Dum Dum" (Roy 113). Taken by itself, the phrase "Dum Dum" conveys a feeling of finality and portrays the seriousness of the situation. However, looking at the phrase in the context of the novel, the reader is forced to acknowledge that it is the same phrase that is in Rahel's version of "Popeye the Sailorman." Because of its origins in the song, the phrase carries with it a lightheartedness that starkly contrasts against the seriousness of Estha's situation. That this phrase that adds humor to the children's song is found at the end of this passage is unacceptable and cruel. It is a deliberate defiance, for its placement dramatically portrays the loss of a child's innocence after he has been exposed to the cruel world. Estha had gone outside of the theatre so that he could joyfully sing a song from "The Sound of Music" in peace without disturbing anyone, but instead of experiencing the expected joy and delight from singing, he encounters Fear. What was lost that day can never be recovered. Thus, it is a statement about the cruel, corrupt world that steals away the innocence of its children. It is in this word that Estha suffers, an unsympathetic world in which while a child vomits out of disgust and fear, his mother ironically is smiling from pleasant dreams a few doors down the hall.

The two narrators also differ in that while one grows in maturity and knowledge of the world, the other remains stagnant. The last paragraph of Benjy's section begins as follows: "Father went to the door and looked at us again. Then the dark came back and he stood black in the door, and the door turned black again" (Faulkner 48). The simple structure, limited use of modifiers, and limited vocabulary characteristic of the style of Benjy's section at the onset of the novel are still present in his narration at the end of his section in the novel. That his writing style has not changed shows that his level of maturity and knowledge of the world have not increased in any way.

In contrast, the changing use of language and depth of insight of the narrator in The God of Small Things signal to the reader that the narrator has matured as a result of the events of the novel. An example of the changing use of language and development of insight is in the use of the phrase "Dum Dum" to signal that a lesson has been learned. The first time the narrator uses the phrase outside the context of the Popeye song is when the narrator responds to Ammu's question of whether Rahel had learned her lesson yet. The narrator answers: "Rahel had: Excitement Always Leads to Tears. Dum Dum" (Roy 94). The first lesson learned is one of books, but as the story progresses, the "Dum Dum" phrases are encountered after life lessons are learned. For example, when the twins discover Sophie Mol is dead and come to the realization that they might go to jail, that realization is followed by a "Dum Dum." And again when they witness the bloody death of Velutha, they learn two lessons: one, that "Blood barely shows on a Black Man (Dum Dum)," and two, "It smells though, sicksweet. Like old roses on a breeze (Dum Dum)" (Roy 293). The shift in placement of the "Dum Dum" phrases from after book lessons to after life lessons shows that they are acquiring more knowledge of the world and are becoming more mature. Moreover, this growth can also be seen through a comparison of the interpretations offered by the narrator of the same scene at different points in the novel. Towards the beginning of the novel, the twins witness a scene where a policeman taps the breasts of Ammu with his baton. The narrator responds by saying that "Inspector Thomas Mathew seemed to know whom he could pick on and whom he couldn't. Policemen have that instinct" (Roy 10). The twins only see that the Inspector is humiliating their beloved mother, and so they think that the policeman is mean. However, when this scene is revisited later on in the novel, the narrator states:

Later, when the real story reached Inspector Thomas Mathew, the fact that what the Paravan had taken from the Touchable Kingdom had not been snatched, but given, concerned him deeply. So after Sopie Mol's funeral, when Ammu went to him with the twins to tell him that a mistake had been made and he tapped her breasts with his baton, it was not a policeman's spontaneous brutishness on his part. He knew exactly what he was doing. It was a premeditated gesture, calculated to humiliate and terrorize her. An attempt to instill order into a world gone wrong (Roy 246).

The later explanation conveys an understanding of society's views and rules concerning the relationship between the Untouchables and Touchables and how their mother had broken those rules, whereas before they had only seen the cruelty of the policeman's action. They are now able to see the action from the policeman's and society's point of view. This level of thought and insight are evidence that the narrator is more mature and knowledgeable of the way that society works. Thus, the narrator has changed from a naive, ignorant child to a person with a more mature mind and an understanding of society.

Trying to find the similarities and differences between these two seemingly different works reminds me of the following quote by Virginia Woolf: "It would be a thousand pities if women wrote like men... for if two sexes are quite inadequate, considering the vastness and variety of the world, how should we manage with one only? Ought not education to bring out and fortify the differences rather than the similarities? For we have too much likeness as it is..." Although this comment refers to the differences between the writing styles of men and women, its message can also be applied to the different cultural writing styles that exist as well. The ability of both authors to utilize the unique qualities of their writing styles to create distinctly different childlike narratives serving different purposes are evidence of their creativity and innovation. As we study the characteristics, purpose, and effectiveness of one writing style versus another, we should also take the time to celebrate the rich diversity and variety in the different language styles that exist around the world.

Works Cited

Faulkner, William. The Sound and the Fury. New York: W.W. Norton & Company, 1994.

Roy, Arundhati. The God of Small Things. New York: Harper Perennial, 1997.

Quiz 1

1. **What town is the primary setting for the novel?**
   A. New Delhi.
   B. Ayemenem.
   C. Kottayam.
   D. Cochin.

2. **What is Kerala?**
   A. The God of Small Things.
   B. The name of Estha's twin sister.
   C. A state in Southern India.
   D. A traditional South Indian form of dance.

3. **What is notable about Roy's diction in the novel's opening?**
   A. It is subtly religious.
   B. It is overtly sensuous.
   C. It is incorrect grammatically.
   D. It makes words shorter than they need be.

4. **What is our first impression of the natural world in the novel?**
   A. It is sexual and rebellious.
   B. It is completely absent.
   C. It is effectively hemmed in by society.
   D. It is quiet and fades away.

5. **What kind of twins are Estha and Rahel?**
   A. Siamese.
   B. Identical.
   C. Fraternal.
   D. Spiritual.

6. **What is unique about Rahel's and Estha's relationship as children?**
   A. They are separated until the age of seven.
   B. They ally with one another against Baby Kochamma.
   C. Rahel is the favorite child, while Estha is shunned.
   D. Rahel can read into Estha's thoughts and experiences.

7. **What incident serves as the focal point for the rest of the story?**
    A. Chacko's divorce.
    B. Sophie Mol's death.
    C. Estha's leaving Ayemenem.
    D. Rahel's return to Ayemenem.

8. **How many years have elapsed since Rahel and Estha last saw each other?**
    A. Thirty-one.
    B. None.
    C. Seven.
    D. Twenty-three.

9. **What is unique about the ceiling of the cathedral where Sophie's funeral is held?**
    A. It is covered with baby bats.
    B. It is treacherous.
    C. It is painted in detail to look like a clear sky.
    D. It is a replication of the Sistine Chapel.

10. **According to Rahel, what is special about Sophie Mol at her funeral?**
    A. She looks English instead of Indian.
    B. She is wearing Rahel's best holiday clothes.
    C. Her body is bloated from being drowned.
    D. She is still alive.

11. **What did Ammu tell the police officer?**
    A. That Babu beat her.
    B. That there had been a terrible mistake.
    C. That Sophie Mol was buried alive.
    D. That Rahel and Estha needed a new guardian.

12. **What did Estha learn to do from a young age?**
    A. Coerce adults into fulfulling his desires.
    B. Make love to a woman.
    C. Go through life unnoticed.
    D. Read his sister's thoughts.

13. What does Estha stop doing as a child?

A. Walking alone.

B. Washing his clothing.

C. Talking.

D. Loving Ammu.

14. What effect does Rahel's arrival in Ayemenem have on Estha?

A. It makes the noise of the world infiltrate his mind.

B. It makes him suddenly remember being molested.

C. It makes him want to run away again.

D. None of the above.

15. What did Rahel study in college?

A. Architecture.

B. Writing.

C. Ornamental Gardening.

D. Communism.

16. Why did Rahel and Larry McCaslin get divorced?

A. Because of a sense of disconnection.

B. Because Larry cheated on Rahel.

C. Because Rahel cheated on Larry.

D. Because Rahel wanted to return to India.

17. What did Baby Kochamma study in college?

A. Architecture.

B. Ornamental Gardening.

C. Communism.

D. Shakespeare.

18. Who was Father Mulligan?

A. A golf instructor at a nearby resort.

B. The patriarch of the Syrian Christian Church.

C. A priest who worked with Baby Kochamma's father.

D. Baby Kochamma's young uncle.

19. **To what length did Baby Kochamma go to impress Father Mulligan?**
    A. She joined the Communist Party.
    B. She swore to convert to Christianity.
    C. She fasted for thirty days.
    D. She joined a convent.

20. **How does the twins' return to Ayemenem make Baby Kochamma feel?**
    A. Excited.
    B. Anxious.
    C. Relieved.
    D. Thrown off guard.

21. **What is Baby Kochamma's relationship to the twins?**
    A. Cousin.
    B. Baby grandaunt.
    C. Baby aunt.
    D. Close family friend.

22. **Who runs Paradise Pickles & Preserves at the present time?**
    A. Comrade Pillai.
    B. Mammachi.
    C. Pappachi.
    D. Chacko.

23. **According to Rahel, what event in the family's history began its strangeness?**
    A. Estha's molestation.
    B. Estha's being sent to live with Babu.
    C. Pappachi's death.
    D. Sophie Mol's death.

24. **What do Baby Kochamma and Kochu Maria have in common?**
    A. They are both Mammachi's daughters.
    B. They have both stolen jewels from the family safe.
    C. They both hate the twins.
    D. They both live sedentary lives and watch television.

25. **What did Estha say when he looked into the face of a "young man with an old man's mouth?"**
    A. "Please."
    B. "No."
    C. "Yes."
    D. "Kerala."

Quiz 1 Answer Key

1. **(B)** Ayemenem.
2. **(C)** A state in Southern India.
3. **(B)** It is overtly sensuous.
4. **(A)** It is sexual and rebellious.
5. **(C)** Fraternal.
6. **(D)** Rahel can read into Estha's thoughts and experiences.
7. **(B)** Sophie Mol's death.
8. **(D)** Twenty-three.
9. **(C)** It is painted in detail to look like a clear sky.
10. **(D)** She is still alive.
11. **(B)** That there had been a terrible mistake.
12. **(C)** Go through life unnoticed.
13. **(C)** Talking.
14. **(A)** It makes the noise of the world infiltrate his mind.
15. **(A)** Architecture.
16. **(A)** Because of a sense of disconnection.
17. **(B)** Ornamental Gardening.
18. **(C)** A priest who worked with Baby Kochamma's father.
19. **(D)** She joined a convent.
20. **(B)** Anxious.
21. **(B)** Baby grandaunt.
22. **(D)** Chacko.
23. **(D)** Sophie Mol's death.
24. **(D)** They both live sedentary lives and watch television.
25. **(C)** "Yes."

Quiz 2

1. **What was the trouble with Babu?**
   A. He abused Ammu.
   B. He did not love his children.
   C. He was a Paravan.
   D. He was an alcoholic.

2. **What did Babu try to get Ammu to do?**
   A. Sleep with Mr. Hollick.
   B. Sell the children into slavery.
   C. Join the Communist Party.
   D. Sell Paradise Pickles & Preserves.

3. **What did Pappachi do to Mammachi?**
   A. Named a moth after her.
   B. Beat her with a brass vase.
   C. Made her work without pay.
   D. Locked her in her room every night.

4. **Why didn't Pappachi get credit for discovering the moth?**
   A. He declined to be acknowledged.
   B. It was classified as a separate species years later.
   C. He did not actually discover it.
   D. Mammachi made sure he did not get acknowledged.

5. **Who told Rahel and Estha about the History House?**
   A. Velutha.
   B. Mammachi.
   C. Ammu.
   D. Chacko.

6. **Why is the family driving to Cochin?**
   A. To march with the Communists.
   B. To ask Murlidharan to become their servant.
   C. To buy a new property for Paradise Pickles & Preserves.
   D. To greet Sophie Mol and Margaret Kochamma.

7. **Who is Vellya Paapen to Velutha?**
    A. His crippled brother.
    B. His boss.
    C. His benefactor.
    D. His father.

8. **To what caste do Vellya Paapen and Velutha belong?**
    A. Brahman.
    B. Paravan.
    C. Kathakali.
    D. They do not belong to the caste system.

9. **Who offered to kill Velutha with his bare hands?**
    A. Vellya Paapen.
    B. Comrade Pillai.
    C. Pappachi.
    D. Estha.

10. **What is Velutha's role in the family?**
    A. Handyman.
    B. Godfather.
    C. Uncle.
    D. Housekeeper.

11. **What does the adult Rahel watch Estha do?**
    A. Urinate behind a tree.
    B. Undress.
    C. Kill ants.
    D. Swim in the river.

12. **Where is Abhilash Talkies located?**
    A. England.
    B. New Delhi.
    C. Ayemenem.
    D. Cochin.

13. **What movie does the family go to see?**
    A. "Babes in Toyland."
    B. "The Sound of Music."
    C. "Alice in Wonderland."
    D. "Mary Poppins."

14. **Why does Estha have to leave the movie theater?**
    A. He wants a Lemondrink.
    B. He cannot stop singing.
    C. He wants an Orangedrink.
    D. He needs to vomit.

15. **What does the Orangedrink Lemondrink man do to Estha?**
    A. He tells him bad secrets about Ammu.
    B. He molests him.
    C. He drugs him.
    D. He makes him promise to bring Rahel to him.

16. **What does Rahel sense about the Orangedrink Lemondrink man?**
    A. That he is a long-lost family member.
    B. That he is The God of Small Things.
    C. That he has wronged Estha.
    D. That he is a good human being.

17. **Why does Ammu tell Rahel she loves her a little less?**
    A. Because Rahel cannot behave.
    B. Because Ammu has a little less love to give.
    C. Because she loves Estha more.
    D. Because Rahel hurt her with her comment.

18. **How does Rachel react to Sophie Mol's arrival?**
    A. She hides behind Estha.
    B. She spontaneously recites a poem in English.
    C. She vomits.
    D. She hides in the window curtain.

19. **To what "Small Thing" does Roy draw our attention on the family's way back from Cochin?**
    A. A jar of illegal banana jam.
    B. A riverbank spider.
    C. A cabbage-green butterfly.
    D. Murlidharan.

20. **What is peculiar about the way the twins read in English?**
    A. They cannot pronounce English words.
    B. They speak with a heavy American accent.
    C. Their pronunciation is uncannily authentic.
    D. They read backwards.

21. **What do we never witness the adult Estha do?**
    A. Take a walk.
    B. Wash his clothing.
    C. Strip naked.
    D. Speak.

22. **Why is it unusual for Velutha to be allowed to play with the twins?**
    A. He was Babu's personal enemy.
    B. He is a man.
    C. He is an Untouchable.
    D. He belongs to the Communist Party.

23. **Where did Ammu die?**
    A. In a hotel room.
    B. In the pickle factory.
    C. In her room in the Ayemenem House.
    D. In the History House.

24. **Why was Ammu cremated?**
    A. Rahel wanted to be able to keep her mother's ashes.
    B. The family could not afford a burial.
    C. The church refused to bury her.
    D. She requested that it be so in her will.

25. Why didn't Rahel write to Estha to inform him of Ammu's death?

    A. She did not know that Ammu died either.

    B. She knew he would already know intuitively.

    C. She did write to him, but he never received the letter.

    D. She hated him for leaving.

Quiz 2 Answer Key

1. **(D)** He was an alcoholic.
2. **(A)** Sleep with Mr. Hollick.
3. **(B)** Beat her with a brass vase.
4. **(B)** It was classified as a separate species years later.
5. **(D)** Chacko.
6. **(D)** To greet Sophie Mol and Margaret Kochamma.
7. **(D)** His father.
8. **(B)** Paravan.
9. **(A)** Vellya Paapen.
10. **(A)** Handyman.
11. **(B)** Undress.
12. **(D)** Cochin.
13. **(B)** "The Sound of Music."
14. **(B)** He cannot stop singing.
15. **(B)** He molests him.
16. **(C)** That he has wronged Estha.
17. **(D)** Because Rahel hurt her with her comment.
18. **(D)** She hides in the window curtain.
19. **(C)** A cabbage-green butterfly.
20. **(D)** They read backwards.
21. **(D)** Speak.
22. **(C)** He is an Untouchable.
23. **(A)** In a hotel room.
24. **(C)** The church refused to bury her.
25. **(B)** She knew he would already know intuitively.

Quiz 3

1. **Why does Mammachi hate Margaret Kochamma?**
   A. Because she is an Untouchable.
   B. Because Pappachi slept with her.
   C. Because things did not work out between her and Chacko.
   D. Because she is prettier than Ammu.

2. **Why does Rahel leave Sophie's welcome celebration?**
   A. To play with Velutha.
   B. To squash ants.
   C. To play with Kuttappen.
   D. To play with Vellya Paapen.

3. **What does Ammu realize when she watches Rahel play with Velutha?**
   A. He looks exactly like Pappachi did as a young man.
   B. She is attracted to him.
   C. He is an Untouchable.
   D. He is trying to replace Babu.

4. **Why does Rahel squash ants?**
   A. It is her daily ritual.
   B. She is frustrated at Velutha.
   C. Estha dares her to.
   D. She is frustrated at Ammu.

5. **Who accidentally insults Ammu?**
   A. Mammachi.
   B. Kochu Maria.
   C. Margaret Kochamma.
   D. Rahel.

6. **What did Estha hide in a pickle jar?**
   A. A secret.
   B. A notebook.
   C. A key.
   D. A mango.

7. **What made Velutha unique in the children's lives?**
    A. He did not judge them or tell them what to do.
    B. He was the only father figure they ever knew.
    C. He hated Sophie Mol.
    D. He did not know how to swim.

8. **Who does not show up on the scene of Sophie's welcome party?**
    A. Sophie.
    B. Velutha.
    C. Kuttappen.
    D. Rahel.

9. **One of Estha's Two Thoughts is "It's best to be prepared." What is the other?**
    A. "The hills are alive with the sound of music."
    B. "Anything can happen to anyone."
    C. "Love laws are meant to be broken."
    D. "Things can change in a day."

10. **What does Velutha promise to fix for the twins?**
    A. A pickle jar.
    B. Their favorite notebook.
    C. Ammu's broken heart.
    D. A boat.

11. **What do the twins plant in the ground when they visit the History House?**
    A. A wooden stake.
    B. A communist flag.
    C. A mango seed.
    D. A Paradise Pickles & Preserves sign.

12. **What does Velutha try to suppress?**
    A. His brother's madness.
    B. A Communist uprising at the pickle factory.
    C. The twins' sexual development.
    D. His growing attraction to Ammu.

13. About what kind of man does Ammu dream?

    A. Paravan.

    B. One-armed.

    C. One-legged.

    D. Much older.

14. What is peculiar about Ammu's interactions with her dream lover?

    A. They never touch.

    B. They are both mute.

    C. They cannot see each other's faces.

    D. They can only swim, not walk.

15. For which of the following does Ammu NOT weep as she looks at her naked body?

    A. The God of Small Things.

    B. Herself.

    C. Babu.

    D. Estha.

16. Who is Kochu Thomban?

    A. A Hindu priest.

    B. A principal Kathakali dancer.

    C. The Orangedrink Lemondrink man.

    D. An elephant.

17. What kind of performance does Rahel watch?

    A. Bengali.

    B. Kathakali.

    C. Koodiyattom.

    D. Westernized.

18. According to Rahel, what do the dancers do when they are done performing?

    A. Swim in the river near her house.

    B. Feed the elephant peanuts.

    C. Go home to beat their wives.

    D. Bathe in ritual oils.

19. **Over what did Margaret Kochamma and Chacko initially bond?**
    A. A bowl of curry.
    B. An academic paper.
    C. A shared love of swimming.
    D. A joke.

20. **What happened to Chacko physically after he finished school?**
    A. He became unhealthily thin.
    B. He became very fat.
    C. He lost the ability to talk.
    D. He lost the ability to walk.

21. **Who is Sophie Mol's biological father?**
    A. Velutha.
    B. Joe.
    C. Babu.
    D. Chacko.

22. **Whom does Sophie consider her father?**
    A. Velutha.
    B. Joe.
    C. Babu.
    D. Chacko.

23. **How do Margaret and Chacko communicate after their divorce?**
    A. By e-mail.
    B. By letter.
    C. They do not communicate.
    D. By telephone.

24. **What image refuses to leave Margaret Kochamma's mind?**
    A. The river in Ayemenem.
    B. Her daughter's corpse.
    C. The History House.
    D. Her husband's corpse.

25. **What did Vellya Paapen tell Mammachi?**

A. That Ammu and Velutha were having an affair.

B. That he was a Communist.

C. That he would never see her again.

D. That he wanted to make love to her.

Quiz 3 Answer Key

1. **(C)** Because things did not work out between her and Chacko.
2. **(A)** To play with Velutha.
3. **(B)** She is attracted to him.
4. **(D)** She is frustrated at Ammu.
5. **(C)** Margaret Kochamma.
6. **(A)** A secret.
7. **(A)** He did not judge them or tell them what to do.
8. **(C)** Kuttappen.
9. **(B)** "Anything can happen to anyone."
10. **(D)** A boat.
11. **(B)** A communist flag.
12. **(D)** His growing attraction to Ammu.
13. **(B)** One-armed.
14. **(A)** They never touch.
15. **(C)** Babu.
16. **(D)** An elephant.
17. **(B)** Kathakali.
18. **(C)** Go home to beat their wives.
19. **(D)** A joke.
20. **(B)** He became very fat.
21. **(D)** Chacko.
22. **(B)** Joe.
23. **(B)** By letter.
24. **(B)** Her daughter's corpse.
25. **(A)** That Ammu and Velutha were having an affair.

Quiz 4

1. **What did Baby Kochamma tell the police?**
   A. That Velutha and Ammu were having an affair.
   B. That she wanted custody of the twins.
   C. That Velutha raped Ammu.
   D. That Ammu was a compulsive liar.

2. **What did Mammachi and Baby Kochamma do to Ammu?**
   A. Locked her in her room.
   B. Beat her with a brass vase.
   C. Sent her to the History House to fetch Velutha.
   D. Locked her in the pickle factory.

3. **Whom did Margaret unconsciously blame for Sophie's death?**
   A. Velutha.
   B. Rahel.
   C. Estha.
   D. Chacko.

4. **Who is "The God of Small Things"?**
   A. Vellya Paapen.
   B. Velutha.
   C. Ammu.
   D. Estha.

5. **What does Chacko do when Comrade Pillai speaks badly of Velutha?**
   A. Promises to fire him.
   B. Storms out.
   C. Defends him.
   D. Tells Comrade Pillai about Velutha's affair with Ammu.

6. **To whom does Velutha go for help after Mammachi fires him?**
   A. Estha and Rahel.
   B. Comrade Pillai.
   C. Ammu.
   D. Chacko.

7. **What does Comrade Pillai notice about Velutha's appearance?**
    A. He is wearing red nail polish.
    B. He is wearing only a loincloth.
    C. He has just been swimming in the river.
    D. He is filthy.

8. **By what is Velutha driven after Mammachi fires him?**
    A. Murderous instinct.
    B. Madness.
    C. His love for the twins.
    D. Instinct.

9. **To where does Velutha retreat after Mammachi fires him?**
    A. The boat.
    B. The History House.
    C. The twins' bedroom.
    D. The Ayemenem House.

10. **Why do the twins run away?**
    A. Strictly for fun.
    B. Ammu tells them they are burdens to her.
    C. They want to get revenge on Baby Kochamma.
    D. In order to scare Sophie Mol.

11. **Why does Sophie Mol accompany the twins?**
    A. They ask her to.
    B. Velutha makes her.
    C. She wants to.
    D. Her mother makes her.

12. **Who tips the boat over?**
    A. Sophie.
    B. No one; it hits a log.
    C. Rahel.
    D. Estha.

13. **What do Estha and Rahel do when they cannot find Sophie?**
    A. Sneak into Ammu's locked room.
    B. Row the boat back to the other side of the river.
    C. Fall asleep on the veranda of the History House.
    D. Walk around the grounds all night.

14. **Who is sleeping in the shadows of the History House?**
    A. Vellya Paapen.
    B. Velutha.
    C. Police officers.
    D. Sophie Mol.

15. **Of whom does Baby Kochamma think when she writes in her diary?**
    A. Pappachi.
    B. Father Mulligan.
    C. Her father.
    D. Chacko.

16. **With what crimes was Velutha charged?**
    A. Kidnapping and murder.
    B. Kidnapping and having an affair.
    C. None.
    D. Murder and having an affair.

17. **Who leads a Communist seige on Paradise Pickles & Preserves?**
    A. Vellya Paapen.
    B. Comrade Pillai.
    C. Velutha.
    D. Estha.

18. **What do the children witness on the veranda of the History House?**
    A. The police beating Velutha nearly to death.
    B. The police pulling Sophie Mol's body from the river.
    C. The police stealing all the furniture in the History House.
    D. The police beating Vellya Paapen.

19. **After they finish with Velutha, what do the police do?**
    A. Beat the twins.
    B. Steal toys for their children.
    C. Give the twins Orangedrinks to calm them down.
    D. Call for Ammu.

20. **What smells "sicksweet, like roses on a breeze?"**
    A. Ammu's old room.
    B. Velutha's blood.
    C. Baby Kochamma's perfume.
    D. The river after it floods.

21. **What does Estha think he is doing when he confirms Velutha is a murderer?**
    A. Bringing Sophie Mol back to life.
    B. Saving Ammu.
    C. Saving Rahel.
    D. Exactly that.

22. **Why does Baby Kochamma pressure the twins into complying with her?**
    A. She does not want to be arrested for filing a false report.
    B. She hates Ammu with all her heart.
    C. She is loyal to the family.
    D. She is under strict orders from Mammachi.

23. **Who tells the twins that they have murdered Sophie?**
    A. Mammachi.
    B. Inspector Thomas Mathew.
    C. Ammu.
    D. Baby Kochamma.

24. **For which of the following is Baby Kochamma not responsible?**
    A. Velutha's arrest.
    B. Ammu's eviction from the Ayemenem House.
    C. Ammu's and Velutha's affair.
    D. Rahel's and Estha's belief that they murdered Sophie Mol.

25. **As adults, what do the twins understand they and Ammu did?**
    A. Ruined their family's honor.
    B. Loved Velutha to death.
    C. Vindicated the Orangedrink Lemondrink man.
    D. Murdered Sophie Mol.

Quiz 4 Answer Key

1. **(C)** That Velutha raped Ammu.
2. **(A)** Locked her in her room.
3. **(C)** Estha.
4. **(B)** Velutha.
5. **(C)** Defends him.
6. **(B)** Comrade Pillai.
7. **(A)** He is wearing red nail polish.
8. **(D)** Instinct.
9. **(B)** The History House.
10. **(B)** Ammu tells them they are burdens to her.
11. **(C)** She wants to.
12. **(B)** No one; it hits a log.
13. **(C)** Fall asleep on the veranda of the History House.
14. **(B)** Velutha.
15. **(B)** Father Mulligan.
16. **(A)** Kidnapping and murder.
17. **(B)** Comrade Pillai.
18. **(A)** The police beating Velutha nearly to death.
19. **(B)** Steal toys for their children.
20. **(B)** Velutha's blood.
21. **(B)** Saving Ammu.
22. **(A)** She does not want to be arrested for filing a false report.
23. **(D)** Baby Kochamma.
24. **(C)** Ammu's and Velutha's affair.
25. **(B)** Loved Velutha to death.

Quiz 5

1. **What do the adult twins do?**
   A. Burn down the History House.
   B. Make love.
   C. Drown themselves in the river.
   D. Sleep holding one another.

2. **Out of what do they do so?**
   A. "Hideous grief."
   B. "Physical pain."
   C. "Mutual understanding."
   D. "Unbridled passion."

3. **On what do Ammu and Velutha focus when they are together?**
   A. Estha and Rahel.
   B. "Big Things."
   C. How to remain together in the daylight.
   D. "Small Things."

4. **Who is Lord Rubbish?**
   A. Vellya Paapen.
   B. Inspector Thomas Mathew.
   C. A spider that Velutha and Ammu watch on the riverbank.
   D. A cabbage-green butterfly.

5. **What do Velutha and Ammu say to one another at the end of each tryst?**
   A. "Someday."
   B. "I love you."
   C. "Tomorrow."
   D. "Small Things."

6. **With what image does Roy leave us?**
   A. The twins making love.
   B. The History House crumbling under its own weight.
   C. Ammu bidding Velutha farewell after a tryst.
   D. Velutha stargazing in the river.

7. **Which scene in the novel did a lawyer infamously attempt to have removed?**
   A. Estha's molestation by the Orangedrink Lemondrink man.
   B. Estha's and Rahel's lovemaking.
   C. Ammu's and Velutha's lovemaking.
   D. Velutha's beating.

Quiz 5 Answer Key

1. **(B)** Make love.
2. **(A)** "Hideous grief."
3. **(D)** "Small Things."
4. **(C)** A spider that Velutha and Ammu watch on the riverbank.
5. **(C)** "Tomorrow."
6. **(C)** Ammu bidding Velutha farewell after a tryst.
7. **(C)** Ammu's and Velutha's lovemaking.

ClassicNotes

GradeSaver™

Getting you the grade since 1999™

Other ClassicNotes from GradeSaver™

For our full list of over 250 Study Guides, Quizzes,
Sample College Application Essays, Literature Essays and E-texts, visit:

www.gradesaver.com

ClassicNotes

GradeSaver™

Getting you the grade since 1999™

Other ClassicNotes from GradeSaver™

The Fall of the House of
  Usher
Farewell to Arms
The Federalist Papers
For Whom the Bell Tolls
The Fountainhead
Frankenstein
Franny and Zooey
Glass Menagerie
The God of Small Things
The Good Earth
The Grapes of Wrath
Great Expectations
The Great Gatsby
The Guest
Hamlet
The Handmaid's Tale
Hard Times
Heart of Darkness
Hedda Gabler
Henry IV (Pirandello)
Henry IV Part 1
Henry IV Part 2
Henry V
The Hobbit
Homo Faber
House of Mirth
House of the Seven
  Gables
The House of the Spirits
House on Mango Street
Howards End
A Hunger Artist
I Know Why the Caged
  Bird Sings
An Ideal Husband

Iliad
The Importance of Being
  Earnest
In Our Time
Inherit the Wind
Invisible Man
The Island of Dr. Moreau
Jane Eyre
Jazz
The Joy Luck Club
Julius Caesar
Jungle of Cities
Kidnapped
King Lear
Last of the Mohicans
Leviathan
Libation Bearers
The Lion, the Witch and
  the Wardrobe
Lolita
Long Day's Journey Into
  Night
Lord Jim
Lord of the Flies
The Lord of the Rings:
  The Fellowship of the
  Ring
The Lord of the Rings:
  The Return of the
  King
The Lord of the Rings:
  The Two Towers
A Lost Lady
The Love Song of J.
  Alfred Prufrock
Lucy

Macbeth
Madame Bovary
Manhattan Transfer
Mansfield Park
MAUS
The Mayor of
  Casterbridge
Measure for Measure
Medea
Merchant of Venice
Metamorphoses
The Metamorphosis
Middlemarch
Midsummer Night's
  Dream
Moby Dick
Moll Flanders
Mother Courage and Her
  Children
Mrs. Dalloway
Much Ado About
  Nothing
My Antonia
Native Son
Night
No Exit
Notes from Underground
O Pioneers
The Odyssey
Oedipus Rex / Oedipus
  the King
Of Mice and Men
The Old Man and the Sea
On Liberty
One Day in the Life of
  Ivan Denisovich

For our full list of over 250 Study Guides, Quizzes,
Sample College Application Essays, Literature Essays and E-texts, visit:

www.gradesaver.com

ClassicNotes

GradeSaver™

Getting you the grade since 1999™

Other ClassicNotes from GradeSaver™

One Flew Over the
  Cuckoo's Nest
One Hundred Years of
  Solitude
Oroonoko
Othello
Our Town
Pale Fire
Paradise Lost
A Passage to India
The Pearl
The Picture of Dorian
  Gray
Poems of W.B. Yeats:
  The Rose
Portrait of the Artist as a
  Young Man
Pride and Prejudice
Prometheus Bound
Pudd'nhead Wilson
Pygmalion
Rabbit, Run
A Raisin in the Sun
The Real Life of
  Sebastian Knight
Red Badge of Courage
The Republic
Richard II
Richard III
The Rime of the Ancient
  Mariner
Robinson Crusoe
Roll of Thunder, Hear
  My Cry
Romeo and Juliet
A Room of One's Own

A Room With a View
Rosencrantz and
  Guildenstern Are
  Dead
Salome
The Scarlet Letter
The Scarlet Pimpernel
Secret Sharer
Sense and Sensibility
A Separate Peace
Shakespeare's Sonnets
Siddhartha
Silas Marner
Sir Gawain and the
  Green Knight
Sister Carrie
Six Characters in Search
  of an Author
Slaughterhouse Five
Snow Falling on Cedars
The Social Contract
Something Wicked This
  Way Comes
Song of Roland
Sons and Lovers
The Sorrows of Young
  Werther
The Sound and the Fury
Spring Awakening
The Stranger
A Streetcar Named
  Desire
The Sun Also Rises
Tale of Two Cities
The Taming of the Shrew
The Tempest

Tender is the Night
Tess of the D'Urbervilles
Their Eyes Were
  Watching God
Things Fall Apart
The Threepenny Opera
The Time Machine
Titus Andronicus
To Build a Fire
To Kill a Mockingbird
To the Lighthouse
Treasure Island
Troilus and Cressida
Turn of the Screw
Twelfth Night
Ulysses
Uncle Tom's Cabin
Utopia
A Very Old Man With
  Enormous Wings
The Visit
Volpone
Waiting for Godot
Waiting for Lefty
Walden
Washington Square
Where the Red Fern
  Grows
White Fang
White Noise
White Teeth
Who's Afraid of Virginia
  Woolf
Winesburg, Ohio
The Winter's Tale
Woyzeck

For our full list of over 250 Study Guides, Quizzes,
Sample College Application Essays, Literature Essays and E-texts, visit:

www.gradesaver.com

ClassicNotes

GradeSaver™

Getting you the grade since 1999™

For our full list of over 250 Study Guides, Quizzes,
Sample College Application Essays, Literature Essays and E-texts, visit:

www.gradesaver.com

470697

Made in the USA